Thomas Howard speaks to all who have ever asked about the apparent impossibility of faith . . . the impermanence of relationships in an anxious society . . . the tragedy of human waste, loss, and misunderstanding. He does not flinch from the hard questions. His answers, drawn from Christianity, speak anew to a troubled 20th century.

"In this book we travel the beaten paths of Christianity, yet here paths so adorned by the author's clear and charming and logical manner that they are made new."
—Dr. Clyde S. Kilby,
Professor of English
and curator of the
C.S. Lewis Collection,
Wheaton College

". . . an excellent book . . . will sell to the C. S. Lewis audience who will find Howard's style and ability delightful. . . . Lewis would be pleased."
—*Christian Bookseller* magazine

Dialogue

Dialogue
With A
Skeptic

(ORIGINAL TITLE: ONCE UPON A TIME, GOD . . .)

by THOMAS HOWARD

TRUMPET BOOKS
published by
A. J. HOLMAN COMPANY
division of J. B. LIPPINCOTT COMPANY
PHILADELPHIA and NEW YORK

DIALOGUE WITH A SKEPTIC
Original Title: *Once Upon a Time, God . . .*

Copyright © 1974 by Thomas T. Howard
All rights reserved
Printed in the United States of America
Published by Pillar Books for A. J. Holman Company

U.S. Library of Congress Cataloging in Publication Data

Howard, Thomas.
    Once upon a time, God . . .

    1. Apologetics—20th century. I. Title.
BT1102.H68   239   73-22213
ISBN: 0-87981-060-2

For my father and mother,
who are separated from each other for the time being
by the Last Enemy,
but who, in their life together here,
taught me and my five brothers and sisters
everything that this book is trying to get at

Preface

It might be a good exercise for all of us if we had the task assigned to us of putting down in black-and-white just what it is we do, in fact, think about things—what we believe, in other words. Most of us, most of the time, operate more or less in a fog, with a few half-specified notions afloat in our imaginations. If we are pressed concerning our ideas, we find ourselves groping for our footing.

The following pages do not, really, present any argument. They represent one Christian's attempt to say what it is that Christians do believe about things. All of it, of course, is entirely derivative. There is not one new thought here. It is all very old. And that is part of the point: I have tried to stay in the path beaten by the historic Church, so that any of the affirmations made would be those held in common by Christians of whatever stripe. I have had the Apostles' and Nicene Creeds in my mind as a sort of touchstone by which to test what I am saying, the idea being that these ancient statements pretty well cover the terrain common to all Christian believers but do not lead us into the brambles of ecclesiology and the finer points of eschatology.

It is an extremely peculiar, not to say baffling, epoch of Church history in which we find ourselves, in that it is widely supposed that *belief* has little or nothing to do with one's claiming the name "Christian." It is (goes the argument) tiresome and embarrassing for Christians to insist that their evangel makes any very bristling claims to historic actuality. It is myth, it is story, it is morals, it is vision, it is style—take your pick: anything that will fit into the ongoing agenda of contemporaneity. God is white, God is black, God is dead, God is where it's at; Jesus is the man for others, he is a revolutionary, he is not a revolutionary; theology is play, theology is dance, theology is visceral, theology is relationship. But: we believe in one God the

7

Father Almighty . . . and in one Lord Jesus Christ . . . Begotten of his Father before all worlds, God of God . . . Who for us men and for our salvation came down from heaven, and was incarnate by the Holy Ghost of the Virgin Mary, And was made man . . . ? Um, hem, well, ah, you must realize that no one nowadays at all supposes that those statements . . . And so forth.

But our fathers in the Church would scratch their heads and look at us blankly. "What do you mean, it doesn't matter? It matters infinitely. You speak of involvement. Involvement in *what?* Why? You speak of style. Style derived from *what?* You speak of relationship. With *whom?* On what basis? You speak of community. *What* community? You speak of celebration. What, exactly, do you celebrate? You speak of commitment. Commitment to what? You've taken up all these large and exciting slogans, and you don't want anyone to press you as to the footing upon which you are moving. But surely—surely, no less than do the Hindus or the Buddhists or the Moslems, you have a *particular* message to announce? Surely your message, of all of them, is the most unabashedly rooted in real, visible history? Surely your evangel is about what *happened?* You do, don't you, have a *story* to tell? Surely the patriarchs and the prophets and the apostles and the fathers and the martyrs and the witnesses and believers down through the millennia proclaimed the Living God, who had a name, and not just style or celebration or relationship?"

And there is the nub. The Christian notion has been that the Word was, in fact, Incarnate. The protagonist in our story is God—God with us. He did not make cloaked forays from Olympus or Asgard; he was born in such and such a year in such and such a village. But at this point we are into the book proper, and this preface has spilled over its appointed bounds.

T. H.

Quod ubique, quod semper, quod ab omnibus creditum est.

I

The Christian thing, really, is a story when all's said and done—a tale. It really could—no, it really does—begin with "Once upon a time." And no matter how complicated you want to make it, you are always talking about a story, with characters and a conflict and an outcome.

If the story is true, of course, we had all better pull ourselves together and find out about it. Even if it isn't true, it is at least interesting. It is interesting not only to fanatics and saints and peasants and ordinary householders, but also to austere and urbane minds and luminous poetic imaginations. The supposition of this book, however, is that besides being interesting, it is also true.

The great difficulty we have about this story's being "true" is that, unlike the stories of Attila the Hun or Atahualpa the Inca, which keep their feet more or less on the ground that we are used to walking on (although admittedly we would not choose to share any ground at all with Attila), this story keeps arriving on that ground and taking off again. It has all the ingredients that we are used to tying up in the "myth" wrapper: traffic up and down the celestial and infernal ladders, and sacrifices, and men blundering into angels and devils, and gods walking along unlikely roads in out-of-the-way places, and dying gods, and (more disquieting) rising gods. This is great stuff for stories, but if it comes down to it, we think we would rather cope with Attila, thank you very much, if you mean that you are talking about things that really happened in our world. This other business is far too jumpy. And besides, we now know that things aren't like that in any case.

Like what?

Angels and gods and celestial ladders. . . .

Oh—right. Now how was it we found out things aren't

11

like that? What was the line of argument that established this point?

Well, science has shown that there is a perfectly natural and regular system that accounts for how things happen in our world, and, as science advances and knowledge increases, the system accounts for more and more of the things that happen—thunder and diseases and all the other things that earlier ages attributed to the gods.

And pretty soon we conclude that it accounts for *all* the data, and hey presto! we discover that the only thing left over as residue to be thrown out is the stuff outside the system—gods and angels and so forth. For one thing, they never show up in the research we have been doing, and for another, all the things the gods and angels were supposed to be doing (cleaving rocks with lightning and healing shriveled hands) can be nicely accounted for in the system.

So far so good. But then a disquieting oddity arises. It appears that once we have got rid of the gods and so forth and each of us is free to chart his own course, we find that the readings we are taking from our chart have led us into the weeds—or worse, onto the shoals. And then it becomes less and less clear where it was we had thought we wanted to go in the first place, and we get a fight over the tiller.

But this was to have been about the story—the one about our world's really being visited by the god. And perhaps right there is the nub. In old tales there were lots of gods visiting this world, but the Christian story, which is still told and still believed by hundreds of millions of people, locates that visit bang in ordinary history and geography. It happened when a particular emperor was presiding in Rome and particular officials and minor kings were running things in the provinces. It wasn't *just* "far away and long ago." Oh, it was a very once-upon-a-time sort of story, but the time was *that year* (when your cousin broke his elbow and when they promoted What's-his-name to captain), and the place was a mile and a half along the road there, just beyond that old hotel Mrs. Thingummy ran for so many years.

Not too much happened, actually. This person was born in a shed back of the inn, and it seems to me that he grew up over in that village not too far from Jerusalem, and then he left home—his father had some sort of shop there, carpentry or leatherwork or whatever—and he went all over the countryside. I'm not too sure what he was doing. Nobody could ever pin down what his thing *was,* but he finally got into trouble with the authorities and eventually they executed him. I felt terrible myself, but there you are. What can you do? I think his mother still lives somewhere not too far from here.

That's not a very good story. I mean, it's boring.

Well, *I* didn't make it up. You asked me if I could remember what the story was, and I told you.

There has to be more to it than that. You're not telling me something.

No, I swear. I was living right here the whole time, and I would have known if anything really exciting had happened. It was all just a lot of running around for a couple of years—people going across the lake to see what he was up to and coming back with stories, and then his troubles with the authorities and that sort of thing.

Well then, what's all the shouting about?

I don't know. You'll have to ask them.

Who?

The Christians.

Who?

The Christians. That's what they call the people who started worshiping him after he was dead. They say he is their God.

Was, you mean.

No, *they* say is.

Mm.

* * * *

That's about how the story would run, give or take a few details. No handsome prince rescuing anybody. No magic spells broken. No kingdoms toppled. No ordeals surmounted. No darkness and terror and victory and joy.

* * * *

Oh, but there *was* a great prince rescuing somebody, and there *were* magic spells broken, and kingdoms toppled, and ordeals surmounted, and darkness and terror and victory and joy.

Well then, you must be mixing up two stories.

No, it's all the one story. The surface events don't give the whole picture. A lot lies behind them. Maybe it's a bit like a report of a surgical operation: One spectator cries, "That man is stabbing that woman!" And he would be quite correct on one level, of course. There are a knife and a wound and blood, and a helpless woman lying on a table, and this big man holding the knife, and a lot of his henchmen surrounding the poor woman. But the rest of us would say, "Yes, but what you have to know is that that big man isn't a monster; he's an angel of mercy, and he is *saving* her."

Oh, rubbish. I can see the knife and the blood. I can see as well as you can. And when I see a knife and blood, I call it slaughter. I'm a plain man, and I don't go for these frills you all tack on. Saving her, my eye.

And you and I would despair of trying to convince the spectator of what was really going on as long as he insisted on limiting the discussion to "what we can all plainly see right there in front of us." We would be pawing his arm and trying to back up to what went before the scene and what would come after the scene and so on.

It's a bit like that with the Christian story. There *wasn't* much to see, and if you drew your conclusions about the whole thing from the plot outline given a minute ago, you would turn away with a yawn.

But the mere outline was only a skeleton, as it were. Oh, it was true enough, to be sure, but it didn't go into the details—and it was precisely those details that worried everyone. Such things as the way the man talked, confounding his critics, driving the moral shaft home again and again and generally leaving everyone agog—or the things he did, splintering the brittle righteousness of the religious officials, comforting the grieving, helping the poor, feeding the crowds, healing the sick, and forgiving people's sins.

Forgiving people's sins? Hold it! I mean, you can't . . .

Well, that's what the story says.

But nobody can forgive sins and all that. Who did he think he was?

God.

Ho ho.

No, really. I suppose we could rewrite the story if we wanted to and say he was only a man, but then that would be our story and not the original one. Surely we have to grant the authors their stories—Homer his *Odyssey* and Shakespeare his *Macbeth*. And the Evangelists their Jesus.

All right, then. I like fiction, too. You were telling me the man thinks he's God and goes about acting like God.

The story is that it really did happen. The fiction we have all dreamed of since the beginning of our myths and our history—the story that all poets and bards and wise men have wished were true—did come true. The god— God, rather—showed himself to us.

And the moon is made of green cheese. We know perfectly well . . .

. . . that that sort of thing doesn't happen in our world.
Right.
Who knows it?
We. The modern age.
Oh. How do we know it?
Because science has proved . . .

. . . that angels never showed up in a lens, and that things happen by natural laws, and that the gods were only wistful and wishful thinking on the part of our poor ancestors. And so no tale of the god—or God—coming to us can be true.

Right.

Well, let me finish the story anyway. The *story* goes that the things that happened were the playing out of the divine drama on the stage of our own history. The boy who was born in a shed back of the inn really was God with us now, once for all, beyond our wildest dreams. And God come not to destroy us, but to save us by taking our flesh—by becoming a man, actually. What the villagers didn't know on the night the boy was born was that angels were singing Glory to God over a nearby field, and that the mother was a virgin (hold it—let me finish), and that already astrologers were en route from some perfumed kingdom in the East, having seen the sign of his coming in the sky. And that what was occurring in a back alley was the thing all their prophets had ached to see, and the whole heaven and earth—all stars and all rabbits—stood on tiptoe to greet.

15

But it doesn't come through like that. I like stories that rise to a real climax and go somewhere. You know—the waif found in the cave turns out to be the prince and drives out the evil king who has seized the throne and marries the princess and so on.

The story does do that.

No, it doesn't; at least the way you tell it it doesn't. It just grinds down to a depressing nonfinish. It never gets anywhere. Nothing catches hold.

To tell it that way is like telling about the Ugly Duckling and leaving out the bit about his turning out to be a swan.

But your story doesn't have any swan or any prince. Your hero just dies, still the Ugly Duckling.

Except that that's not really the end. The hero dies and things go on their merry way. But something has happened. A tiny cloud the size of a man's hand has appeared on the horizon of the kingdoms of this world. Not too many people see it. A few shepherds and fishermen and women, maybe—and, as it turns out, all the hosts of angels and archangels, and the mountains and seas and frosts. Naturally, it escapes the notice of the kings and the philosophers. But their number is up. *Our* number is up. Everybody's number is up.

What do you mean?

That the thing that happened so dully in that tinhorn province of the Empire was the crux of history. Everything that happened before that was emphatically *before* it; and everything that happened afterward was *after* it. The god— God, that is—had really come. . . .

This is just a lot of trumpet-blowing.

You have to watch out for trumpets. The people in Jericho found that out, alas. And the Day of Doom isn't going to be announced by any ukulele, believe me. Anyway, the person the authorities got rid of that afternoon outside the town was God the Saviour of the world.

Saviour? This is getting rhapsodic.

Well, it is rhapsodic, I suppose. That's like complaining to Homer that his story is getting positively epic. Anyway, yes, Saviour. The legal functionaries who OK'd the execution for that afternoon hadn't the slightest idea that they were triggering, you might say, the central episode of the cosmic drama. The thing is, his death was a divine sacrifice —the Divine Sacrifice.

I tell you, this is getting out of hand. You keep taking flight.

I told you at the beginning that the story kept lighting on the earth under our feet and taking off again. That's in the *story*. It's a matter of the biggest things happening huggermugger, like an acorn beginning to push against its shell in the dirt at the corner of your house. Nothing happening here, ho ho ho. Anyway, the death was a sacrifice because the man who was killed was God with us and he walked straight toward that death with his eyes wide open. Not with some frenzied martyr complex, either. It was the finishing of the thing he had been doing all along—the thing he had been born in our flesh to do.

What was he born in our flesh to do?

To share our life and our sufferings and our limitations, and to teach us and show us what real, unspoiled human life looks like, and then to offer that perfect life up to God as a sacrifice on behalf of the rest of us who had botched things. The old prophets had said that he would carry the *sins* of the world. There was a prophet living in his day who saw him and called out all of a sudden, "Behold the Lamb of God, which taketh away the sin of the world!" What a thing to say.

II

Well, it didn't come to much, if you ask me. There's still quite a bit of sin around, if you don't mind my mentioning it. He didn't take much of it away.

Um, I think my example of the acorn might help here. To the man poking around the garden, looking at what is happening there, nothing very earthshaking is going on. No bulldozers, no land mines, everything quiet and safe. Oh, to be sure, there's that little acorn there in the dirt, but it's not worth worrying about. It won't do any harm. The difficulty with the man's grasp of the situation is that the little acorn happens to be oakness in a nutshell. Once that shell has broken open, all oakness breaks loose, and the whole garden is in jeopardy. The Christian story says that an acorn has been planted in our garden.

I'm not sure I follow the connection between this acorn business and the Lamb of God's taking away the sins of the world.

Well, you said it didn't look as though much sin had been taken away. And if the point of the story is that when he died he somehow siphoned all the sins and horrors off of society so that from then on nobody would be cruel or selfish or obnoxious, then of course it's a dead loss. The story is nonsense. The most fanatic Christian can hardly insist that Rome, or even holy Jerusalem, got up the next morning all cleaned up and unselfish.

So the acorn example?

It's this. Something broke through then. The thing the garden was really all about from the beginning appeared, very modestly, at that point. The garden was to have been a garden *for the oak tree,* you might say, but this had been forgotten along the way. And then the thing appeared. There would be a lot of uprooting and pushing and chang-

19

ing before the thing was finished—before the oak tree reached its full growth. But all that would be a matter of the garden's becoming what it had been designed to be. The point of the comparison is only this: The Christian story says that the seed planted on that miserable afternoon near Jerusalem was a sort of beginning. It was the seed broken open. Now all oakness is upon us, and everything is going to be uprooted.

And the Lamb of God? We have a confusion here, what with lambs and acorns. . . .

It's not as bad as it looks. The acorn business was just to try to get an example of a big thing that starts in a rather small and unpromising way. The Lamb thing was to get a picture of that death as not just a butchery, but as a sacrifice. Lambs had been used for thousands of years for that purpose and, according to the story, this particular death was *the* Lamb, whose offered life answered before God for men's sins.

What an outrageous notion! I mean . . .

You mean that to us civilized and enlightened moderns it looks bloody and barbarian and grotesque. Of course it does. *Reality* would look bloody and barbarian and grotesque if we took a hard look at it. Anyway, the notion was that in this death the thing that had occurred, strange as it may seem, was the offering up of a life—*the* life—in behalf of the whole world. Except that it was our own life—our own flesh—and not mutton that was offered up as a sacrifice.

But what was the point? *All this business of* sacrifice *just doesn't ring any bells nowadays.*

Well, I don't know. There are various ways of stopping the sound of a bell, of course. We can stuff our ears with cotton, or we can stuff the bell with cotton. We might look to our ears and our belfries before we complain that the bells don't ring.

Let's suppose it is about something important, then. What is it?

It's that we needed a sacrifice. There was a breakdown between us and God, and the ancient notion is that if there is this sort of breakdown, you forfeit your life.

Hold it. How can there be a forfeit like that? That's a grim kind of game, isn't it? Here we are, playing the game, and the first time you make a mistake you get the ultimate forfeit.

Would that it were a mere mistake. The story has it that it *wasn't* a mistake; it was a choice. You and I, or Adam and Eve (it comes to the same thing)—all of us, in other words—made our choice. The rule of the game was that the players had to obey the king. We dumped it in order to get the thing we thought we had been denied.

You're going to say freedom, I bet.

Mm. We *thought* it was freedom, but we had it backward. We thought freedom meant that everyone could act like the king—or God, say. So we started acting as though we were gods—beings who do whatever they please. But that was all wrong. We weren't gods; we were creatures made by God for God, and hence our real freedom was quite literally a matter of choosing obedience to him. It sounds like a paradox because it is. But it's a deep one, and we didn't want any part of it. We wanted self-determination, or autonomy, and the only way to get that was via disobedience. The trouble was, since the very nature of the game involved the mystery of freedom-via-voluntary-obedience, to change that formula, which we did in Eden, was to try to redefine everything, and we have carried the confusing, horrifying consequences ever since. It would be a little like angels demanding roast beef, or clams wanting to fly. Both claims would cause confusion, and both would lead to frustration and rage if they were insisted on. Anyway, we broke the rules of the only game there is; and since it *is* the only game, the stakes are everything, and we forfeited everything, in effect.

I still say it's a pretty grim game.

Maybe so. *I* didn't make it up, though. And remember, when you are playing a game with God, you can hardly expect meager rewards and petty penalties. Since it is about everything, the rewards and the penalties are as big as the takes. However, there's another equally ancient notion in there: even though the forfeit was total, somebody else could undertake the forfeit. One life could be offered for another. In old ceremonies this was usually signified by using a domestic animal—a lamb, say. The loss was carried by the lamb.

But that's a charade! It's just another game.

Maybe it could be seen the other way around. Maybe all our games are little piddling echoes of the way the whole thing really *is* organized. Maybe there really *are* rules and forfeits and rewards and so on. But anyway, as you say, it was a charade in one sense, since of course no mere lamb or heifer could really take away somebody's sins.

Why did they go through with it then? It certainly was distasteful and expensive.

They went through with it because they knew they were playing out the opening moves in the real game—the one where the real Lamb would be offered. The deadly serious one that you and I are head over heels in, whether we like it or not.

Well, I'm not in it. Leave me out of this.

You were asking what the story said. This is what it says —that the death of that man there that afternoon was the Sacrifice for the sins of the whole world.

What did he do? Just appoint himself the world's lamb?

No. He was appointed.

By whom? Some committee of the whole?

No—by God. He is called "the Lamb slain from the foundation of the world." I tell you, this story brings you up against it—I mean, everything in time and eternity comes to a point in the events of this story. The onlookers see this and that happening, and the story says yes, but what you see has all this behind it. The onlookers see a pregnant girl, and the story says that she was a virgin and that there was an angel who brought news to her that her child was the Son of God. The onlookers see a local feast and the mysterious replenishing of the wine supply, and the story says that the Son of God was the guest who was responsible. The onlookers see a sad death, and the story says that man there was the Son of God and while it was quite true that he was convicted and executed by routine procedures, it also happens that his death was his offering himself to God in behalf of us men—us sinful men.

But it doesn't seem to be a very auspicious business. It ends so miserably.

So goes the onlookers' account of the events. Probably a few of them would recall that there was some flap a day or two later—people running about and soldiers being investigated on charges of being asleep on duty and so forth. The report got around that he had risen. No doubt his friends made off with his body—that sort of thing. And the *story* says that all the hurrying in and out of the burial place was how the Biggest Thing Ever appeared on our stage. *It* had happened.

What had happened?

The Kingdom of Death had been invaded and toppled. He really *had* risen.

Oh. So there is *a bit about kingdoms toppling, eh?*

If you can call the toppling of a kingdom of that magnitude "a bit," yes. The story tells us that behind the spectacle of that death and burial, huge struggle was going on.

Between what and what?

Between heaven and hell. Light and dark. Good and evil. God and Satan. Freedom and bondage. Joy and wrath. It says that the man dying there was the Prince of Glory, waging war on the Prince of Evil.

A minute ago he was a lamb.

He has a long list of names and titles. Prince and servant, warrior and peacemaker, priest and sacrifice, shepherd and lamb, husband and brother—these titles all give us some hint of what he is. In this case, he is the lamb in his offering himself for us, and the prince in his waging the fight for us. Either way, it is a matter of delivering us from slavery—from death, really. Our lives were forfeit to death, says the story, and hence we were in the clutches of death. The sacrifice and the assault were the same thing. The sacrifice *was* the assault.

What do you mean? How did this great struggle, as you put it . . .

The story goes that in these events—this death and burial—the precincts of hell were invaded and toppled. The dying man was really the Prince of Glory entering the fray himself, and dying, and by that death destroying death.

How?

The story doesn't say *how*, any more than your biography will one day tell us *how* it came about that a purely biological event resulted in this intelligent spirit called You. We never get the secret of how the pumpkin is turned into the coach. We never find out exactly how the egg becomes a feathered swan.

Well, what did he do, then?

He fought—he was our Champion, you might say—against death and hell, which would destroy us. He carried the fight right onto the enemy's own ground, and beat Death by breaking out of its power. Nobody had ever done that. There was now a way out. He broke the spell for us by bearing our flesh right through the precincts of death and right on out again. That's why we can speak of that Sacrifice and the fight as the same thing. By submitting to death, he overcame it. We all went in with him, as it were, and came out with him.

Who?

Anybody who would follow. Actually, that's what happens to a person who does follow him: he finds himself being led on a path that goes bang through death and out again.

III

So then everybody who had died before this assault took place was out of luck?

No. From the very start there had been a rumor of a coming deliverer—a champion. He was looked for. And so when he came and won the fight, his victory gave us an entry through the Gate of Life whether we happened to come through the story before this chapter or after it.

Who started the rumor?

God. The story goes way, way back—to the beginning of things and beyond that. What it's all about, really, is this great and good Lord whose own people were hell bent to get out from under his sovereignty, and how he did everything imaginable to woo them back to him—sent signs and various warnings to them, and messengers, and finally his own son. It was a shabby picture.

But if they wanted to get out, why not let them out? After all, we hold these truths to be self-evident, et cetera. People have the right to liberty and the pursuit of happiness in their own way. He should have let them go.

He did, in a way. He certainly didn't flog them back in. The thing about it was, though, that he wasn't just some petty neighborhood baron. He was the Lord of everything there was, and the only alternative for his people (besides obedience to him) was slavery.

I don't follow you. If he had let them go, they could have learned self-determination and responsibility and so on.

That's a nice idea, and we'll probably keep up the attempt to prove that it's true until the Falling Tower crashes down on us. But the story says that obedience to this Lord equaled real freedom, and that the effort to achieve freedom by getting out from under that obedience ran us straight into slavery—abject slavery—and the worst sort of tyranny—the tyranny to our own whims and desires—and that this ran us swiftly into frenzy and boredom and impotence.

Well, I don't think I agree.

Not many people do. Nonetheless, that's what the old story says. Of course, you have to remember that the Lord was an entirely good and wise Lord. They all knew that, but they kept forgetting it, or finding other things that looked more alluring. Ordinarily this effort of theirs to get out from under was simply a matter of wanting some other lord, or else of wanting no lord at all. Just self-determination, to use your word.

I'm not sure I follow how we arrived here. How did we start talking about disobedience to this Lord when we were talking about death?

The disobedience *was* death. That's the alternative. The point is, remember, that this Lord was the Lord of everything there is. He had, um, *made* it all, as a matter of fact. It was his kingdom. All the exits from his kingdom led to darkness and havoc and fury and despair, and he knew this, so of course he greatly desired that his subjects continue to enjoy the light and order and joy of his kingdom. But there was this oddity: He was an absolute Lord—no mistake about that—but he was not a tyrant. You were *allowed* to go if you wanted to. The exits were there. Most of them were terribly attractively painted and gilded, too. There were promises and invitations stippled and filigreed all over them. But it wasn't as though he didn't keep telling his people that this was all a lie.

I could have told him that he'd have problems with that kind of setup.

I suppose I could have, too, if he had asked me. But the point was, he wanted a kingdom populated by people who were choosing to obey his rule rather than by a horde of serfs or thralls. He was no pharaoh.

You still haven't explained to me the connection between getting outside his gates and death.

It was just that the terrain outside was under another lord, an evil and greedy lord who spent his whole time in the effort to subvert the Good Lord's kingdom. His policy was to lure as many people as he could out to his kingdom and then enslave them. His slavery was synonymous (literally, I mean) with death, since it reduced you eventually and utterly to something you were not: a thing, a rag, a shard. You entered it all bright-eyed and bushy-tailed, lured by sweets and ices and fragrant syrups, and you ended up an unnoticed residue. Almost nothing.

For heaven's sake, if it was that bad why didn't this Good Lord just go out and overthrow his evil neighbor? I mean, it doesn't seem very intelligent or noble . . .

Mm—no. One of the things about this Good Lord is that he keeps his own counsel. He is exceedingly mysterious. All his counsels are wrapped in enormous mysteries. What comes *through*—or what you can see—is good, of course. His subjects will tell you that—that he is good and merciful and generous and loving and wise. But if you were to press him with questions about why he doesn't do so and so, you would get stony silence.

That seems a little austere.

I don't suppose anyone who has ever had any dealings with him would say that he was *not* austere—frightening, even. The people who know him best sometimes use the word "terrible."

But about this overthrow . . .

Yes. The thing that had happened, apparently, was that all of us—I mean all the people in the Good Lord's kingdom—had opted out. They had the idea that things would be better if they chose their own set of rules, so they did, and, since another set of rules means another lord and another kingdom, they presently found themselves out there. But it turned out, as I say, to be an exile and a horror. The evil lord wouldn't let them go back.

And the overthrow?

The Good Lord came and broke the evil lord's tyranny and opened the gates back to his own kingdom. They could get back in now.

Why didn't they all come trooping back in, then, if the other was so horrible?

Well, it's a slow business. The drama doesn't unfold in a minute. For one thing, of course, the horror of the outside kingdom didn't necessarily come over them all at once. Things were quite pleasant just outside the gates, actually. But once you got there, you were kept moving farther and farther away from the walls, and you found the grass turning to flint underfoot, and the syrups turning to brine. You kept going—or rather you were kept going—until you found that the only way to describe the landscape was to call it hell, and the only word for what had happened to you was death. But you weren't permitted to reverse direction. That's what the Good Lord did, though: he broke that spell. You could turn around.

If this "outer kingdom" you're talking about was such an enormous cheat, I still don't see why the Good Lord allowed it to get going in the first place, or why he didn't just wipe it out and close his gates so that nobody would even run the danger of getting out there.

You've asked The Question about the whole story. There's no answer, if what you want by way of answer is a log of the Good Lord's reasons for doing what he does. The most the story implies is that it all has to do with the particular sort of place his kingdom is and the sort of people who are at home there.

What sort of kingdom is it?

It's a kingdom of liberty. Nobody is bundled or dragged in. The people who live there have been invited in, or called in, or helped in, or whatever. But nobody is there who would just as soon not be there. It's the Kingdom of Love.

Oh. That sounds awfully nice.

No, really, it is. The Lord of the kingdom is Love himself. And the kingdom is populated by people who have been changed by love—or are being changed, let's say. Changed, actually, into what they were meant to be to begin with but had ruined by breaking the rules.

You mean that by breaking the rules they lost love?

Yes.

I don't get the connection. How can you lose love by breaking rules?

It's not that hard to grasp if you remember that the rules in the first place were a sort of exact description of love. I mean, all the dos and don'ts added up to a way of living that puts the person first. And that's what love is. You know—the rule "thou shalt not" do so and so could be rephrased "love doesn't" do so and so.

Hold it. Love is a feeling. Love is spontaneous; it has nothing to do with rules.

I'm not sure you quite meant that. If I poke the man who has insulted me, that is certainly spontaneous, but it's hardly love. And all the things you see going on in sandboxes and playgrounds—the squalling tugs-of-war for shovels and nasty exchanges of taunts—those things don't have to be taught. They're spontaneous. They're natural. But they're not love. It's an almost impossible job to teach somebody to respond in a different way. Contrary to what we like to tell ourselves, love is not "spontaneous" at all. It has to be learned. And the rules are the cues.

But how can you say love isn't spontaneous? You don't have to teach a baby to love its mother, do you? You don't have to learn to fall in love.

Of course not. And aren't those two examples precisely elementary forms of the bigger thing that love really is? A baby's "love" for his mother is the same thing as his need for her, isn't it? She is his world. She gives him everything—food, warmth, security, comfort. His love is wholly selfish in one way, but we applaud it because it is a beginning step in his journey toward love. He is getting his first lesson in what trust and happiness between two beings mean. His is the easy part in this lesson, of course; his teacher (his mother, that is) is doing all the giving. But it's only the first lesson. Later the lessons become harder: His natural family loyalty and affection for his sister, say, are tested in the playroom, and the rules are hard there. "You must let *her* have the Tinkertoys now." But we try to get him to see that the "rules" are only signposts pointing him in the direction of love—that is, the state of affairs where he is asking "What can I do for her?" rather than shouting, "Hey! How long is she going to get to play with them? I want them back."

And later, the experience of falling in love is a wonderful emotional experience of a state of affairs where giving yourself for another person is joyous. The lover doesn't have to be coerced into doing things for his lady; he wants to. Giving to her, and giving himself for her, is his greatest joy. So that this particular lesson in love—this "falling in love"—is speeded along, or gilded, we might say, with an emotional bliss. It really is bliss to do things for her. The man in love isn't forever asking what his rights are in this relationship. As soon as that word appears between them, we know something has gone wrong. Now they're coming back down to earth and having to come to terms with ordinariness. But even there I think we'd see, in a real love match between two people, not a draining off of this romance into squabbles about rights, but rather a ripening and deepening of that initial romantic passion into quiet habits of giving and kindness and courtesy and so on. Love hasn't fled. It's the noon—or the afternoon—of love, you might say, rather than the hilarious dawn. What was new and promising and exciting back there has become stable and habitual and quiet.

That's a very long speech you're making. What happened to the story?

Ah—the story. Yes. You were asking about this kingdom, and about how love and rules could be so mixed up with each other. And I was just trying to show you, from an everyday example, how that is. The "rules" for playrooms, and for marriages, and for societies, and for nations in their dealings with other countries, are only efforts to fix and describe what love would command anyway. "Thou shalt not" can always be reworded to say "love doesn't." Try it. "Thou shalt not kill." Now you say . . .

Love doesn't kill.

Bravo. Now once again: "Thou shalt not steal."

Love doesn't steal.

By George, he's got it! Well, as I was saying, this kingdom is the place where the rules have been learned and have long since disappeared. The self-giving demanded by the rules has now become habit, and, lo and behold, the people have found out that the habits aren't dull and gritty but blissful. The "What can I do for you?" thing has long since replaced the "Hey, I want that!" thing, and it turns out to be sheer joy.

I don't see it. I mean, a person has to protect his rights, especially when there are that many people living together.

But if all the people have let their claim to their rights die, there are no rights to protect, are there? Or at least no quarrel. All this calculating and tallying things up and squinting over equality and so on are swallowed up in joy.

It's all too visionary for me. You can't bring about a state of affairs like that. It's a mad dream.

Let's just say that this mad dream is what the story says the kingdom is really like.

But I don't get the connection between this part of the story—the happy citizens of this blissful kingdom all having learned an impossible lesson and having been changed into a completely new kind of people—I don't get the connection between this and the earlier part where the Lamb offered himself for them and the Prince of Glory fought for them.

It's not too remote a connection, really. In fact, the connection is quite clear, if you think about it for a second. When we were speaking about him as the Lamb, the point was that his offering of himself was *for them*. And, by the same token, his fight as the Prince of Glory was also *for them*. In other words, what he did—however you think about it—was in our behalf.

Their behalf, you mean. We're talking about the story.

Well, anyway, the story says that what he displayed was love. It is love, isn't it, that displays this sort of self-giving? It's the opposite of snatching and quarreling and shoving. He laid down his life, really. And they were the ones who benefited. It was because of what he did that they could enjoy deliverance and liberty.

And the connection between this and the rules?

Isn't it just that what he did not only brought about their being delivered and restored to his kingdom, but also demonstrated to them the pattern of the way things are in that kingdom? And the rules are a kind of exact itemizing of the same thing—of the way things are in that kingdom.

Such as?

Self-giving. Laying down one's life for the other. The Lord of the kingdom does it and shows the way to his people. The rule of the kingdom is self-giving. You first. My life for yours. It's called love.

Oh.

And the rules are the first steps—the tutors, as it were—to spell out how love operates. It doesn't come naturally. Everyone learned habits of quarrelsomeness or selfishness or timidity out in the bad lord's kingdom, and they all passed them on to their children, and it's a long, slow business to win through to the free and joyous state of affairs in the Good Lord's kingdom. That's what the rules are for—to start the process of learning. Practice excercises. They itemize for us . . .

Them.

. . . for them the way love works. But the Good Lord *enacted* it for them. They could see it before their very eyes, not only in that final, great self-giving when he offered himself up for them, but also in everything he ever did. It was a nonstop matter of self-giving all his life long. Actually, it *started* with a great act of self-giving.

What do you mean?

He emptied himself of his glory and majesty when he came to them. He became one of them. To rescue them, he came to their aid, not by sweeping in with clouds and fire and trumpets and drums, which a great lord *could* have done, one would think, but rather by quietly and unostentatiously becoming one of them. He went among them out there in their exile and lived with them and helped them and told them in the simplest possible language what had happened and what his kingdom was like. And he invited them back in.

It still doesn't seem the most efficient way to me. He could have done it all with one swat, if he was as great as you say.

Except that that would have been a contradiction. Remember, his way was a my-life-for-yours way. So, if we're talking about efficiency (although he's not a production analyst, he's the *Lord*), you might almost say that the best way to get through to the people with exactly the message he wanted would be to *show* them the message—to act it out for them, to have a display. You know—show and tell.

Ah. So he was acting out the my-life-for-yours way?

Right. He waded into the bad lord's kingdom, if you like, bringing his own kingdom with him. Like the acorn in the garden almost—the seed of the thing, the promise of the new thing. But not *simply* the promise; more than that, the thing itself, right bang in the middle of them.

So what happened?

What you would expect. It was such an obvious and stark contrast that naturally comment was aroused, and some people were attracted by it and began to be convinced, and others hated it or were frightened. There was a full-dress division of the house—a war, really.

It's an odd war, with one side offering to lay down its life for the other.

It *is* an odd war. It got down to a grim struggle between the Prince of Darkness (that's one of the names of the bad lord) and the Prince of Glory. But the Prince of Glory beat him by being defeated.

Hold it . . .

No, really. That is the one stratagem the Dark Lord's kingdom cannot cope with.

What?

Self-giving. Love. It is absolutely fatal. The whole thing tumbles down. It was the strategy that the Dark Lord could not foresee, since it was the one thing that did not, and could not, ever exist as a possibility in his realm. He had no way of imagining it.

So what did he do?

He killed the Prince of Glory—or thought he did.

I thought you said the Prince of Glory beat him. Besides, when you were talking about the Lamb, you said it was voluntary. You can't "kill" somebody who's determined to die, can you?

That's another oddity in the story. The death was both the worst and the best thing. It seemed to be victory for the Dark Lord and defeat for the Good Lord. But it was absolute victory for the Good Lord and total defeat for the Dark Lord.

I don't see how he defeated the Dark Lord if he died in the combat.

Remember, death is the ultimate weapon of the Dark Lord—the thing to which all his strategies lead. And if that weapon is ruined, the whole strategy collapses.

And the Good Lord . . .

. . . ruined Death by breaking out of it. He went into that last prison and broke it open. By the sheer might of his love, he broke the tyranny of the Dark Lord's kingdom, displaying right in the middle of it what his own kingdom was like, and then, as if his words and his life among the people weren't enough, finally dramatizing it by the ultimate example of what he was talking about. He had *talked* about my-life-for-yours as the Way and had shown it to all

33

of them in a thousand ways in his own day-to-day life. But now he summarized the whole business by really giving his life for theirs. And with that, the evil spell was broken. The tyranny of evil was overthrown, and Death was ruined.

IV

In other words, this whole thing that he was doing—his coming to them to begin with, and his dying and rising, as you say—was a matter of showing them a way and then making that way possible.

M-mm. And of course it wasn't just a way *out;* it was a way *in.* Out of death into life. Out of bondage into freedom. Out of falsehood into truth.

What do you mean, falsehood?

Well, the whole kingdom of the Dark Lord is a cheat. It operates on fraud.

How?

Good heavens—how else could he operate it? How could you lure anyone into that kind of tyranny without making it look pretty inviting on the outskirts? Sodom always looks like fun on the outside.

Sodom?

You know—the promise of lots of fun and instant goodies anytime you call for them.

What's wrong with that?

Only that that way of going about it ends up with boredom and solitude.

That's hard to believe. I mean, Sodom was noted for allowing pretty free and spontaneous personal relationships, wasn't it? A life like that wouldn't be boring or lonely.

But the whole thing operated on a how-much-can-I-get principle, which is exactly the opposite of the idea at work in the Good Lord's kingdom.

I still don't see how that leads to boredom and solitude.

Well, follow it for a minute: If your relationship with somebody has been a matter of getting what you can from him, pretty soon you're going to get all you want from him and start looking for fresh supplies from somebody else.

35

People become mere merchandise to you—mere way stations on your quest for pleasure. And once you're functioning on a people-as-merchandise idea, you become harder and harder to satisfy, and what you are looking for in them becomes narrower and narrower, and "relationship" has long since gone out the window.

Um . . .

And your quest becomes more frenzied and more bleak, and finally you wake up one fine day and discover that you have turned yourself into the sort of monster who only *devours* people and is beginning to find even this fare unsatisfying.

That's a rather extreme picture, isn't it? I mean, I know plenty of people who go after what they want in life, and use people for their own selfish purposes, and they end up pretty well satisfied.

"End up" is saying too much too soon, isn't it? You don't in fact know *how* they *end up*. We're all making ourselves into one sort of being or another all the time, and we can't see the end of the story yet.

And speaking of the story, how did we get off here? You were talking about Sodom and saying that the Dark Lord's kingdom is a cheat.

Well, it is. The same thing would be pretty vividly illustrated anywhere you look; for instance, the way selfishness makes monsters out of us and eventually drives us into solitude. While we were in the middle of it, it always looked like the search for the good thing—the thing we wanted: Turkish delight; the secret garden; the pot of gold. But it's like the egg that eluded Alice in *Through the Looking-Glass*—always just beyond our fingertips.

I'm not sure yet that I see the connection.

Just this: the people in the Dark Lord's kingdom find themselves lured by the promise of something very desirable, and set about to grasp it, and it always eludes them somehow. Eventually their entire attention becomes fixed on what they want, and by that time they find that they have arrived at a flinty desert where there's no question at all of getting what they set out to find. And there's no one to turn to, since their companions on that way have all been pursuing *their* own quest and nobody has established any sort of bond with anyone else. Everybody has merely *used* everybody else, and they end up as a scattering of solitary and angry exiles. They have been defrauded.

What is it they're lured by that eludes them so dreadfully?

Anything. Anything they want. Some nice taste or smell, or some sort of landscape. Or power, maybe. Or safety. Lots of times it's nothing worse than that.

Safety?

Mm. They just want to be safe from everybody else. They don't want to be bothered or to bother about anyone else. Anyway, the point is that the great Fraud waits greedily for the people in this kingdom. Death, I mean.

What waits for the people in the Good Lord's kingdom?

Life. Joy. Utter joy. That's what the promise is.

I see—the promise. But the other kingdom holds out a promise, too. How on earth is a person supposed to decide between two promises if both sound so good?

He'd have to look at who is doing the promising. Actually, that's the Good Lord's condition: you follow him out of the Dark Lord's kingdom and into his on the supposition that what he is saying is true.

But then that's just a choice between Tweedledum and Tweedledee, isn't it?

I suppose you might say that, at a glance. But heavens— not really. It turns out that Tweedledum and Tweedledee (your example, not mine) aren't at all alike. Oh, they do look alike for a bit. That's part of Tweedledee's game. He's an unbelievable mimic—a copycat. He can dress and dance and sing and juggle almost exactly like Tweedledum. And in some ways he beats Tweedledum.

How?

He's more lavish at handing out goodies sometimes. He has endless supplies of goodies. Tweedledum seems a little stingy now and again. But they both promise everything.

So why should anyone ever choose Tweedledum?

Because he—let's call him the Good Lord—promises life and liberty and joy to anyone who will follow him out of the Dark Lord's kingdom, just as the Dark Lord promises life and liberty and joy to anyone who will stay with him. So it looks like a draw—a flat option. But it isn't that neat, because if you listen really carefully to what each one of them says, it is perfectly obvious who is telling the truth. The things the Dark Lord promises are clearly fraudulent.

What do you mean?

Well, the whole way of doing things in his kingdom leads straight toward hostility and competition and isolation between people—everyone after what he can get, grabbing for the best seats, snatching the biggest doughnut. It all leads to a squabble, and to people plotting against other people in order to do them in. The idea that the Dark Lord encourages is: Get the best. Get it no matter what. Look out for Number One. That's the only way to secure happiness. Obviously, this is no scheme for a joyous society. It sets everyone against everyone else.

What's the alternative?

The opposite. The Good Lord's way. My life for yours. You first.

But that's no good. I mean, it doesn't sound very attractive to me. Maybe for a lot of masochists it is, but ordinary people want a little pleasure and a little independence and so on, and realize that you have to go after them. This business of making a doormat out of yourself—you can keep that.

It isn't that, really. It's a matter of taking a hard look at the way things are—the way things have to be—and seeing which set of cues leads in that direction. The Dark Lord's cues imply that everyone else is in your way, standing between you and fulfillment. The Good Lord's way is that by abandoning your own private quest for "fulfillment" and by giving a hand to this person over here, and that person over there, your own fulfillment comes over you from behind, gloriously and dazzlingly. It overtakes you. You get to point A by heading toward point Z. You find it by not scrabbling for it.

How do you do that?

It's a sort of paradox, really. But it's the same paradox that was at work in the Prince of Glory's conquest of death. It was via death that he won life. Or, put another way, the road to life lay through death. It's true all up and down the line, from that huge struggle between the Prince of Glory and the Prince of Darkness to the humdrum choices that present themselves to us a thousand times a day.

You mean I always have to choose what I don't want in order to guarantee that I'll get what I do want later?

Um, no. It's often a matter of refusing the immediate and apparently obvious gain in favor of the more solid—and maybe more remote—one. It's a matter of taking up the discipline that the Lord prescribes; namely, the training of yourself to pursue it *his* way and not your own. Your own inclinations nudge you along one way—"Get it! Grab it! Do it! Have it!" and so on. His way says, "Death to all that. Real life stands on the far side of this death. Don't grab the instant goodies. Don't hug a bogus safety to yourself. They are fraudulent. Open your hand; drop that fake pearl. The Pearl of Great Price is over this way. Seek *it*. Go after *it*. Sell all that you have and find it."

But that looks like a contradiction to me. You don't go after it, but you do. You get the pearl by pretending not to look for it.

It is a paradox—there's no avoiding that. Maybe you can see it this way. It's the difference between the long view and the short view. The Good Lord holds out the promise of life on the far side of death, or of a real fulfillment as the culmination of a discipline designed to lead you to that goal. It's a little like athletics maybe: The pole-vaulter can execute the beautiful pole vault because he has submitted to the particular disciplines designed precisely to achieve that particular kind of mastery. In order to get there—to win through to the beautiful and joyous ability to do that particular thing—there were plenty of times when he had to choose the long view (mastery at pole-vaulting next month) over the short one (chocolate éclairs and beer this afternoon). It was a sort of death. You could find examples of the same sort of thing anywhere you want to look. Music, for instance. The violinist can play the marvelous and difficult. Bach partita because he has practiced the disciplines that lead straight to that kind of mastery. The mastery and the excellence are one thing there, and the ability and the joy are one. What began as a matter of slogging along has now flowered into a mastery. And the mastery isn't something different from the discipline. It is exactly that discipline burst into flower. The master is putting his fingers on the strings in exactly the same places as the beginning pupil is, but he's doing it unconsciously. And it be-

39

comes a means of joy for the rest of us. What began as drilling and tears and vexation for the unhappy little boy who would rather have been out in the mud puddle is now a means of joy for him and the rest of us. We all benefit from his death.

His death?

It comes to that. The long view over the short view. Bach ahead of the mud puddle. It was a sort of minideath for him on that afternoon when he had to forgo the mud puddle. The joy of the thing wasn't very apparent at that point. The pearl, if you like, was his mastery of the violin, and he got it by giving everything to that pursuit. If somebody came along and convinced him to forget the Bach and go ahead and enjoy the mud puddle, we would have objected that that person was cheating him.

Am I to gather, then, that it's always a matter of choosing the grim and tedious thing over the fun and games?

No, no. If we left it with those examples, I suppose it would look that way, but it's not at all that bleak. The starting point is to settle it quite soberly that one will follow the Way, and it is the way of life-on-the-far-side-of-death. But in practice it's not *merely* a matter of sprints versus éclairs, or Bach versus puddles. It's simply that whatever choices one *does* make are governed by obedience to the rule of the Way. In the early stages one may be conscious of being a bit out of breath and of wanting éclairs when they're not always appropriate. But as time goes on, the realization begins to dawn "A-*ha*. So *this* is what it's all about? By Jove, this is a jolly sight better than getting fat on éclairs. This is the real thing, it is, it is. Now I'm beginning to see what they're talking about. Now I'm beginning to learn what I was made for."

OK, I can see that. But how does all this furious personal discipline tie in with the whole idea of the Kingdom of Love that the Good Lord is supposed to have opened up to us? I mean, love is something that involves more than one person, and you're talking about some ferocious program of purely personal discipline.

It's not as remote a connection as you think. The "discipline" is all a matter of getting us out of ourselves—of changing the direction of our efforts, you might say, from grabbing to giving, from in to out.

40

What does that have to do with love?

Everything. I mean, my natural, untrained inclination is to grab. Oh, it may be gentle and civilized and respectable grabbing, but still, my inclination is to make sure that I get what is owed to me. That is natural, and it's pure Dark Kingdom. It drives wedges between me and my fellows and arouses quarreling and fighting. So that, if there is a state of affairs anywhere where the opposite thing is at work—where it is a matter of giving out instead of grabbing—I'll have to learn it. And the giving out is what goes on in the Kingdom of Love. They know how to do it there. It's swift, joyous speed. In the Middle Ages they thought of it as a dazzling, twinkling dance performed by myriads of creatures who have learned the steps.

Hold it. You're flying off again into rhapsodies, and all I asked was what these personal disciplines have to do with the Kingdom of Love.

Sorry. Although it does come to that, you know. A dance, especially a complicated one like this one, is carried out by pure mutualness, you might say. That is, I give way as you advance, now the other way, now back again, and so on. As soon as a person decides to go it alone and do his own thing, the pattern is fouled up. His steps may be an intriguing personal display, but if they aren't governed by the rules of the dance, you end up with a brawl. Nobody knows what to do. But I guess the immediate connection between the personal discipline and the Kingdom of Love is that I have to learn to love something besides myself. There has to be something greater than me and my wishes in my vision.

Why?

Because it's a *kingdom*. It's not a clutter, or a cacophony of private individuals each shrieking and struggling for his own rights; it's a kingdom—a structured, ordered, joyous whole. And to have that, the individuals in it have to have learned that there is precisely a whole that is bigger than any one of them, and that it is a whole to be loved.

So they have to love the kingdom?

Yes. And more than that.

What?

It's the King, really. That's where the love begins. It's a command.

A command? You can't command love.

Not the feelings of love, no. But if love is really this matter of putting something or someone else in front of myself, it can be commanded.

I don't see why it has to be anything so grim as a command.

Commands aren't necessarily grim. I mean, "Forward, march!" isn't grim if the platoon is headed toward the gate and freedom. And for another thing, it may take a command to boost us off dead center. Otherwise, we might spend our whole lives luxuriating in questions and discussions and so on as to what might be the best thing to do, and generally enjoying the state of doubt and paralysis. Whereas the command breaks in and says, Get *on* with it. And, being a command, it is itself a pretty vivid cue about the whole business.

How?

Just this—it places obedience and choice and action in front of us rather than feelings and talking and so forth. I mean, it's great fun if you can sit around chatting about the great quest for truth. But you can't do that in the Good Lord's kingdom. At least, that's not what the kingdom is all about. It's a much more prickly business than that. You have to do something.

What?

Love the Lord your God—the King.

Hold it . . .

No. That *is* the starting point. He insists on it.

Who?

The Lord.

But I can't just start loving him presto chango.

I don't suppose anybody would argue that you can work up a warm or soaring feeling about him. But that's not what the command is about in any case. It's a matter of beginning by choosing to make him your God. Your highest good. By settling it quite clearly that to know and obey him is worth more than all other possibilities put together.

But why should I do that? How do I decide that this alternative is better than any other?

I'm afraid it doesn't come to us that way. It's not a matter of one of several possibilities being held out to us so that we can mull over which lord we'll choose. Oh, of course, there is a sense in which that is the picture, to be sure. No one is knocked on the head by the Lord. It is a "choice" in the sense that disobedience is a real option. But that's the point: it is a question of obedience or disobedience, rather than a neutral choice like the choice between peaches and pears.

Suppose somebody prefers the other lord? I mean, there are two lords, aren't there?

Not really. There is only one Lord, and he is the Good Lord. The Dark Lord's lordship is a cheat. He is no lord at all. He isn't the "other" lord, if by that we mean that he and the Good Lord divide up the sovereignty somehow. He will, of course, be your lord if that is what you choose, but it will turn out that you have chosen a cheat, an illusion. It's no more an equal alternative to the Good Lord's lordship than death is an equal alternative to life, or darkness to light, or a vacuum to air. All of these, I suppose, are "alternatives" in some sense, but nobody will argue that they are on a par with each other. Life and death aren't Options A and B like peaches and pears. It's more like peaches and fake peaches. That would be a set of alternatives, in one sense, but only in some mocking sense. If a peach is the real thing, then a fake peach, although it may look and feel like a real one and appear to promise all that a real one promises, is no alternative. It's a mockery.

V

But how is one to reach this place of deciding to choose the Good Lord if the peaches and the fake peaches look so much alike?

The Lord calls to us . . .

But so does . . .

. . . the other lord. I know. But the Lord God calls us with the voice of truth and authority and love. It is a matter of obeying a call rather than weighing an ambiguous choice. It is begun with his summons to us. He has sought us, not we him. That was the whole thing in the story—his coming to us to seek and find and rescue and set us free. It isn't presented as a matter of two neutral options.

So let's say somebody does respond to this call, as you put it. Let's say I do make him my King. Where are we then?

Well, I guess you could say it's a bit like a birth—or a death, rather. I mean . . .

Hold it. I must say, if it's a question of not knowing whether it's more like birth or death, I'd just as soon avoid the whole thing. Anything that is so confused that you can't tell whether it's . . .

Wait. I think I can show you what I mean. The Christian story is full of that very birth-death mix. In the ceremony that marks a person's beginning in the new Way (it's called baptism), you have it: the death is the birth. The end of the old way of evil is the beginning of the new life—a burial and a rising to life. The one is the other. Really, I suppose when you get down to it, any birth is a death for the person involved, and vice versa. Take physical birth. Think what a frightful trauma it must be for the poor baby: this is the end—the nice, warm, safe, quiet, comfortable world is all of a sudden being shattered, and I'm being

45

forced out of the only life I have ever known—oh, help!—ouch!—Lord, save me!—what's happening?—oh, no—cold air—horrible hands gripping me—they're thrashing me now!—this is intolerable! And the rest of us would be hard put to it to convince the subject of all this pulling and hauling that it was anything other than death. But we insist on calling it birth, and we, from our vantage point, know that in fact it does usher the subject into a new world that he had no way of imagining. And, parenthetically, the Christian vision would see our physical death that way. From this side of the line, it looks intolerable. It is the end: the complete interruption of everything, the failure of everything, the tearing of the fabric of life to tatters. Pain, sorrow, gloom, silence, the end. Oh, horror. But, says the story, that's only what it looks like from this vantage point.

Now you're about to give me some shimmering, hazy picture of death as really being a matter of soaring off into the summery blue—that sort of thing.

No, not quite that. The Christian story doesn't pretend to give us any very clear and exact pictures of what happens at death. But the one solid expectation that *is* held is that death is not the utter end. Its crushing sovereignty has been snapped, and it is to Life that we go upon our exit from this stage. To God. To our real home and our real, solid identity and joy and freedom.

Mmm. But we were talking about this other birth-death business—when a man begins on the Way, as you put it.

Yes. When you begin to follow Christ . . .

What? How did we get here? You said "love God" a few minutes ago, and now you suddenly substitute "follow Christ." You're forever slipping new things in. I must insist that we . . .

. . . stay on the track? You were asking about the Christian thing, and for Christians the business of loving God and following Christ is the same thing.

Now wait. You can't tell me that a man has to follow Christ in order to love God.

I'm speaking about the Christian thing, remember. And the story there is that God—the only God there is—the everlasting Father, the Almighty, the Creator, the King of kings, the Blessed and Only Potentate . . .

Steady.

Right. That this God has, in fact, disclosed himself to us in the middle of our own history, our own life. His name, when he walked among us as a man, was Jesus. Jesus *is* the Christ—God's holy one. He spoke the words of God to us. He *was* the Word of God, and he exhibited to us what God is like and what God wants of us. The God that he disclosed to us is the God whose name is Love, and the first command of this God is that we love him. We find out how to do that by looking at his Christ, and by listening to his words, and by picking up and following him. Loving God and following Christ are the same thing.

Oh.

At any rate, this beginning, or whatever we want to call it, is like a birth in that it is just as important an event as our physical birth, to say the least. Jesus used that picture, actually. He called it being born again.

You are not going to tell me . . .

. . . that a man can enter into his mother's womb a second time and be born again?

Right.

You ask good questions. There was a man of the Pharisees named Nicodemus . . .

What?

Sorry. I'm just quoting. He's the person who first asked your question. Anyway, the answer he got, straight from the Incarnate Word's mouth, was that a man did, in fact, have to be born into the new life as literally as he was ever born into this planet.

So it's a matter of entering upon a new life. But then what's this death business?

I suppose it's just what death is anywhere: the end. In this case, it's an end of the old way—the way of the world. The ways of my natural inclinations. My gut reactions. You know: competitiveness, shoving into line, envy, cruelty, laziness, vanity, fear, unconcern—the whole scene. Self-centeredness, in a word. The beginning of the new means the death of the old.

Wonderful. Let's just make the big transaction right here and now, and everything will be set. I'll be scot free from all my besetting sins—all my vices. Whoopee! Instant sainthood! Although, come to think of it, I'm not too sure that sainthood is exactly what I want at this point.

There's no great immediate danger, actually.

Pshaw.

It's a pretty slow business. The same sort of thing as the acorn and the oak that we were talking about awhile back. The new thing begins. It is there, living and growing and taking over. But oh, dear—the growing pains, and the tempests that rage over the poor little sapling, and the weeds that clutch and drag at it.

More rhapsodies. What are you talking about?

It's just that this new life, this hauling the sails about and beginning in the Way of loving God instead of ourselves first, this following Christ, is a big enterprise—a long, slow one—and not always entirely easy.

How long and how slow?

At least as long as your time span here on this planet, and maybe a lot longer than that. And as slow or as fast as you want to make it.

But why is it such agony?

I didn't say it was agony—although no doubt there's plenty of agony in the process, just as there's plenty of laughter and joy and everything else. Really, it's exactly like life, mainly because it *is* life. It's what human life is all about.

What is human life all about?

Becoming what we were meant to be. Growing up into our real wholeness instead of wasting our time and shriveling up. It's a matter of getting on with the serious, exhilarating business of human life rather than chasing after fox fires.

Fox fires?

You know—all the things that lure us off. Success, power, prestige, pleasure, popularity, revenge, self-determination—that whole bit. All those things that make us slaves to frustration, competition, fear, jealousy, envy, humbug, posing, and so on.

You make it sound so dire.

I suppose it is dire, if you want to put it that way. I mean, if the stakes are really either ultimate freedom or ultimate slavery, I guess one could say that it is important, if not urgent, if not dire.

But why is it such an operation?

That's a little like asking why the leveling and rebuilding

of Manhattan Island would be such an operation. I mean, if you want to redo something completely, it usually turns out to be something of an operation, doesn't it? In this case, it's the complete redoing of a person. Me. You.

But I don't see what's so terribly wrong with me (or you for that matter). I'll admit I can do with a little touching up here and there—rough edges and all that. But that's more of a polishing operation than a total redo.

Mm. I suppose that by some ordinary everyday accounting neither of us shows up too badly. Nothing too shocking. But the difficulty is that we're not being subjected to any ordinary everyday accounting. It's an extraordinary ultimate accounting. We're being measured up against the perfect standard.

Hold it. Whom are we being measured by, if you don't mind my asking?

God.

Oh.

Seriously. We're not being asked whether we stack up more or less evenly with everyone else. We're being assessed against the stature of the Perfect Man.

Who?

Jesus Christ.

Now wait. That's not fair. You said Christians believe he is God. Well, to measure us up against God and do us in because we don't show up very tall—it's not fair.

Except that the great thing about him was that he was really, truly, literally a man. He wasn't God in a costume; he was a man. He had emptied himself of his divine prerogatives so that his human life wouldn't be an empty charade. The human perfection—what you and I are measured up against—was just that: *human* perfection. Actually, this gets you into some big stuff, according to the story. It's as if the whole human race is set forth in two representatives and we're identified in both of them.

What two representatives?

Adam and Christ. The idea is that in the story of Adam you see acted out what every single one of us since then has done anyway—chosen our own will in preference to the will of God. The story of Eden has teeth in it for that very reason: it's the story of my life, to coin a phrase. Adam (the human race—me) has gone his own way, and everything is lost. But there was a Second Man, so to speak—the man who did it right. The human figure who acted out the drama of perfect obedience to God, as a perfect son obeys his father, and who thereby won everything back. And the figure that we're judged against is this Christ—the only wholly free and good man ever to appear in our history. If you want a depressing exercise, start lining yourself up beside him. Listen to his words. You'll find yourself quickly heading for a hiding place under the nearest cabbage leaf. It has a dwindling effect on a man.

How do you mean?

Just the obvious. We don't show up very *tall* against the standard. Or put it another way: the kind of human life Jesus Christ exhibited in front of us makes our ordinary way of doing things look pretty tawdry.

You're always talking in generalities. How does Jesus show us up?

How? He keeps driving to the heart of things, and he always seems to find the soft place where it hurts. He reasserted the old Law, for one thing, except that he made it more ferocious than ever by insisting that the area of conflict between good and evil is not merely in external acts— you know, whether or not you actually *do* knock somebody on the head—but inside us, right in to our *inclination* to knock somebody on the head. Attitudes. He insists on impossible things, such as not getting angry, and not lusting, and giving to anyone who asks, and loving your enemy.

Well, you can't expect people not to have normal reactions to things. I mean, anybody is allowed a little resentment, for instance.

Um. No, in a word. At least not by this standard.

Well then, the standard's too high for us mortals. It has nothing to do with ordinary human life. It's absurd.

You may be right. But the whole point of the entire business is that *Perfection* has invaded "ordinary human life," as you put it, and that now everything is up for grabs. We haven't been left alone with our ordinariness. We've been *bothered*, if you like, by Perfection—by the Kingdom of God. So that it's no longer a matter of ordinary human life. The whistle has been blown on that, and the call has sounded to extraordinary human life. Real human life. Human life as the King of Love originally designed it to be.

Oh, boo. There you go taking off into rhapsodies again. You do that when you don't have anything else to say.

The difficulty about trying to stay down on the meat-and-potatoes level that you'd like to keep it on is that the meat-and-potatoes situation has been drastically changed by something from outside. The trouble is that the Kingdom of Love has been announced and exhibited and planted in our midst. In the middle of our ordinary life, with its ordinary, "excusable" reactions, another Way has loomed that places all this ordinariness and excusableness under condemnation.

Hold it. Condemnation? Who's condemned for ordinary little faults?

You. Me. You'll accuse me again in a second here of flying off into the wild blue yonder, but *I* didn't make this all up. The Christian thing sees hell yawning just beyond our little "excusable" ordinary reactions.

OK. First it's Perfection, and now it's hell. Ultimates under every bush.

I'm afraid there are.

Are what?

Ultimates under every bush. Because the whole point of what Jesus Christ was getting at was that these ordinary, commonplace attitudes and exchanges and reactions and choices—little strike-backs and bits of gossip and tiny underminings of somebody else, and resentments nursed along and daydreams of getting the edge on somebody—all these things bubble up from the black fountain called self-centeredness. Every droplet of irritation and revenge and lust and so forth comes from somewhere, and it most certainly doesn't come from the fountain of love.

Well, there's no sense in my even starting on this Way that you're talking about if it's going to be a matter of fussing over every teeny reaction I have, and of coming to a dead halt over the thousand and one ordinary human reactions in the course of every day. Good heavens—I should think a man had a right to spout off once in a while, or indulge in a few lecherous daydreams. Your way looks like a surefire setup for a nervous breakdown to me.

I suppose it might look that way from the outside. But it's not as though it had never been tried. The plain fact is that ordinary mortals, as well as saints and philosophers

51

and poets, have tried it, and have found what they call freedom. To follow this Way is to find yourself moving farther and farther into the territory of freedom. It's a matter of being increasingly set *free* from the tangle of these things.

But I just can't see it. It simply does not follow that if you start creeping along, scrutinizing every single little motive and attitude and reaction in yourself, you will find yourself in this great freedom. You'll never make me believe that.

You're leaving out one tiny thing, though. Nobody ever claimed that it was a matter of creeping along. A better way of putting it would be to say that you are following a Guide through all sorts of terrain—rocky ascents, green glades, city streets, plains, highlands, bogs, and so forth. But through it all runs a path.

Where to?

Freedom. Life. Joy. It's not a matter of coming to any halt over trivial things. It's more a matter of increasingly getting free from a lot of chains, you might say, so that you are freer and freer to get on to where you are going—freer to be yourself.

Chains?

All these "ordinary human reactions." We flatter them when we call them that. They are really chains. They are forged at the anvil of self-centeredness.

A couple of minutes ago they were droplets from a fountain.

Touché. It's just another picture—like one of Aesop's fables. In one fable you're a hare, in another a mouse, in still another a hen, and so on. It's just a way of getting at something that's true. Anyway, these things—all this irritableness and worry and timidity and sluggishness—are really like chains shackling us down and weakening us. But in following the Guide—let's face it, in following Christ—you find them loosening and snapping and dropping off. It's not a matter of sitting down and scrabbling at them, hoping they'll break before your fingernails do.

Well, I don't see how it works.

Nobody does, really. There's no mechanical chart with arrows and Tab A in Slot B and so on that shows you exactly how it happens. But the fact is that by listening to his words and by obeying his commands and by keeping your eyes on him, you do, in fact, begin to move along the Way. And—you have to change the picture again to get another thing in—what is really happening is that you are *living* in him.

Mm. I'm sure.

He talks about himself as a vine. Our relationship to him, as well as being like a follower and his guide or a servant and his lord and so on, is like a branch and the vine. The branch lives in the vine. It gets its life from the vine. Jesus used that picture. So that really the changing and energizing process comes flowing up into the branch from him.

Hurray. There's nothing to do but relax. Just let the old sap flow in. Automatic sainthood after all. Painless transformation. Instant perfection.

Instant nonsense. I said that's one *picture* of it. And it's a true picture, of course. What it comes down to is that from *our* angle it is a matter of setting out on the way of obedience—of making a perfectly serious effort to live up to his words and his example. But what is happening all the time *in* that effort is that he himself is living and working in us and bringing about the transformation. He promised his followers that that is what he would do.

Oh. So I'm to conclude that Jesus has taken up his abode in me somewhere. Let's see now—where would he be most comfortable?

Watch it. You're talking about one of the Big Things.

What thing?

The Holy Ghost.

Help!

That's an old name for him. I just thought I'd jolt you. He . . .

It.

No, he. He is God with us now. He is God in the world, calling men, nudging men, watching over history, and living in his people. Jesus told his followers that when he went away from them after his Resurrection he would send his own Spirit to live in them, to be his presence with them even more intimately than when he was here in the flesh.

That's all way beyond me. I'm sorry—I mean, you can't expect anybody who isn't a saint or a theologian or something to get into all this.

Maybe not, if "getting into all this" means just talking about it and trying to unscramble the mysteries. But that's not what it comes to for Christians. It's like your lungs and air: neither you nor I is either a pathologist or a chemist, so we don't have too much to say on the topic Lungs and Air. But we *breathe* now and again.

Mm.

That's not a bad picture, come to think of it. There are lots of things like that. The *explanation* throws you, but the thing itself is something you count on and act on all the time. Gravity, electricity—that sort of thing. For a Christian, the Holy Ghost—or the Spirit of Christ—is God in us. He's the one who brings the whole thing to pass.

What whole thing?

Bringing us to our real freedom—to the thing we were made for and had lost by our disobedience: identification with Christ.

Identification with Christ?

Yes. That's actually the goal—to make you and me into perfect men. Free men. Whole men.

What's that have to do with identification with Christ?

Because he's the perfectly free and whole man. He is the image of what a man really *is,* untarnished and uncrippled by evil. It is to the freedom and wholeness manifested in Christ that we are being brought. The Bible talks about being made into the image of Christ, or growing up into Christ, or reaching the measure of the stature of the fullness of Christ. It's a tall order, but rather exhilarating when you think about it.

Fine. But I'm not a candidate.

Why not?

It's too far beyond me. Really, I must say it seems to me that your whole notion of this thing is much too inflated. Can't God just accept me as I am, just little me? I'm not out to do anybody in or organize any anti-God putsch or whatever. I'll settle for just living my life and doing what I can in my own little way. Good grief—why does it all have to be so enormous?

I guess everybody would like to know that. But the bleak and glorious fact is that it *is* enormous. It *matters.* It matters infinitely.

What matters?

You, in a word. Me. Everybody. The universe isn't indifferent. It's not an ordinary, business-as-usual sort of universe. Christians believe that Love, and not mere force or something, is at the bottom of it, and Love doesn't leave you alone. It matters infinitely that we respond to that Love. It—or he, rather—won't leave us alone until we have responded. It's not nothing that we're up against; it's God. It's eternal Love. We can't go on pretending that it isn't so important after all, and that we can dodge the big issues by settling into the cocoon of just-living-my-life-and-doing-what-I-can-in-my-own-little-way. Good heavens, man, if it matters enough to *God* that he went through *death* for us, I'd say it's worth sitting up and paying attention to.

Well, I just don't think I can cope with all that. I'm no theologian.

And I'm no pathologist.

And I'm no candidate for sainthood.

Why not?

Because I can't do it.

Neither can anybody else.

Then what are we wasting our time for?

Because there is grace.

Who?

Grace. *It.*

What's grace?

It is God's own sufficiency channeled to us to bring us along in this business of becoming whole. It is his help given to us to make up the lack left by our weakness and imperfection. It is his life, really, coming to us day by day. If it weren't for grace, the whole thing *would* be a farce, as you say.

But what does it do?

It begins to make real inside of us what the whole story talks about outside of us. We're not left gaping at an unreachable thing. God has come to us, and his Kingdom has been announced and displayed before our very eyes, and we are invited to citizenship in that Kingdom. But we're not left alone to try to beat our way along toward that impossible standard of perfection. As a matter of fact, that impossibly high standard is itself planted in us. Soon it begins to grow and take over, somewhat like the acorn—in fact, exactly like the acorn. Just as the acorn was planted in our history, you might say, so it is planted in our own selves. The same seed. The Kingdom of God. New life.

New life? But how . . . ?

The business of being at home in the Kingdom of God is so far beyond anything we can ever begin to hope to achieve that we may well throw it all over in despair. The people who are at home there are either a completely different kind of creature to begin with than we are or else they have gone through a naturalizing process that our imaginations boggle at. How in the world am *I* supposed to get to the point where I am at home with people like Saint Francis and Saint Paul and the Virgin Mary?

Oh, good heavens. I've already told you, I can't . . .

That's probably exactly it. Good heavens. It *is* good. It *is* heaven, eventually. But it's not too easy to start feeling at home there. It demands all you've got. However, help has been sent.

What help?

The Comforter. The Holy Ghost.

What's this grace, then, that you were talking about?

Maybe one way of putting it would be to say that it is what God offers to us of himself. The story says that it was by his grace that we are freely offered new life and citizenship in his Kingdom of Love, and it is his grace that is channeled to us by his Spirit. Really, it's not so different from what the word means anywhere else.

How?

Well, anybody knows what "grace" means when you are talking about a woman or a gymnast or a giraffe or a porpoise. It has something to do with beauty and harmony, and with a thing's being easily and magnificently itself—doing perfectly and effortlessly what it seems to be designed for. I should think that's not a bad picture of what God's grace is. I mean, this breathtaking offer of life instead of destruction, of freedom instead of slavery, and so forth, is a pretty vivid disclosure of God. It is God doing his thing, to borrow a phrase, perfectly and beautifully, in the same way that a gymnast or a porpoise does *his* thing. It is God being what he *is*.

But how does that fit in with whatever this "grace" is that you say works in us to bring us along the Way?

It's the same thing, isn't it? Isn't it God giving himself to us, in effect, to bring us along in the Way of learning to give ourselves, since this self-giving is precisely the beauty and perfection and joy that his Kingdom is all about? Or look at it the other way around: all sorrow and despair and anger are eventually a matter of self-giving's having broken down somewhere along the line. All cruelty and fraud and spite and so forth—all the things that spoil joy and beauty —are reverses of self-giving. And the thing that God offers to us in our getting on toward the goal is grace—his self-giving. Maybe it's a two-fold thing. It's both an example and an assist. It is the example of what God is like, and it is that Godlikeness made available to us to help us along the Way.

So how do I connect up with this grace?

Well, there are various means. There is, of course, the fountainhead which is God himself. It is his Spirit—the Holy Ghost—who brings everything from God to us and makes it real *in* us. And there is his Word.

What's that?

His Word. The Bible.

Oh, dear.

Why oh, dear?

I had a feeling you would bring up the Bible sooner or later. I mean, it's good stuff and all that, but it's not really something that attracts people like me too much. It's so connected in my mind with childhood and Sunday school that I can't get worked up about it

Mm. I know what you mean. But it is a peculiar book, really. It keeps escaping everybody's efforts to get at it.

How?

Well, it seems to exist in a category by itself.

Oh, I don't know. There are lots of holy books and scriptures around. The Bible certainly doesn't have any corner on that.

No I suppose it doesn't have a corner on being some-body's holy book. But it's an extraordinary book. There are a lot of moral teachings in it, and wise sayings, and a good bit of poetry, but the overall thing is a narrative. It's a story.

I thought there were a lot of stories in the Bible.

There are. Lots of them. But it's all one big story, actually.

Of what?

Of grace.

Grace?

Yes. God seeking man. God coming to man.

You've got it backward. Religion is man's search for God.

On that definition, the Bible isn't a very religious book, and Christianity is no religion. You'll have to scratch hard in the Bible to find much about anybody seeking God. Oh, they do, of course. But the way the stories go, it always turns out to have been God who sought them first. The man seeks God and finds him, and then finds out that he has been found by God. It's a little frightening.

Am I being looked for by God?

I should think it's a fairly safe bet that you are—if you're a member of the human race.

But what does this Bible business have to do with the means of grace?

It's the Word of God.

Oh.

Really, it is.

Magic, eh? A magic book.

No more magic than anything else around. If you mean "mysterious," then yes, very mysterious—just like everything else in the Christian thing. How was Jesus God and man at the same time? How can anyone have a virgin mother? How did Jesus rise from the dead? It's a little like that with the Bible. It *is* what anybody says it is—a collection of a dozen different kinds of writing from a dozen different centuries by X number of men, all of them with a limited viewpoint. And God only knows (literally I think) how the whole thing was put together. All told, it looks like the biggest paste-up job ever. But it holds together. It's life-giving. It's true.

But I still don't get the connection between the Bible and the means of grace.

It's pretty simple, really. Christians say that by reading the Bible they are helped along their way.

What do you mean? Little golden thoughts for the day and that sort of thing? "Be ye kind," and "I will lift up mine eyes," and all that?

All that and a lot more. It's nothing mechanical. It has

something to do with just plain learning and obeying, of reading about what God is like—what he has done—and of being ready to step along in the Way that's pointed out. You read these hundreds of stories about Adam's encountering God and what happened, and about Noah and Abraham and Moses and Joshua and David and Solomon and Ruth and Esther and the rest of them, and you find that you are looking into something that's big and true and demanding.

Now hold it. How am I supposed to get anything out of some story about Joshua? Am I supposed to get a trumpet and march around the walls of Chattanooga or Muncie seven times until they fall down?

Who knows? Although that would hardly seem likely. It's more a matter of finding out what sort of God it is who is spoken of in the Bible. What was the experience of this man, and this one, and this one? What did God ask of him? Of them, really: it was a whole people he was calling to himself, to show them his ways—ways of mercy and justice and truth—and all these stories add up to a pretty vivid picture of who he is and what his ways are like and what he is asking of us. The whole collection sets the standard, you might say, but it also plants and waters that standard in us. The Bible doesn't just shout at us from the top of some hill and say, "OK, everybody! Here's what God is like! Here's the list of demands! Get on up here!" It's more like food, giving us strength for a journey.

I thought you said it was a means of grace.

I did. The Bible *is* one of the means of grace. *How* that poetry, and those wise sayings, and those stories come to life in us and strengthen us and begin to transform us is no clearer than how a piece of beef or a bowl of raspberries enables us to get on with life. The mysteries are pretty similar, really. One way or another, there's a leap in there you have to make in your explanation, from beef to energy, from Joshua to holy living.

Holy living? Who's talking about holy living? You're going to be trying to get me into sandals and a cowl in a minute.

Um—that's not required dress, actually. And "holy living" isn't some special category for hermits and grizzled

59

monks. It's just another name for this whole business of learning what it's all about.

What what's all about?

Life. Authenticity. The Kingdom of Love. The Kingdom of God. The business of shifting over from the Dark Lord's kingdom to the Good Lord's kingdom. From the way of grabbing to the way of giving. From saying "My will be done" to saying "Thy will be done."

And the Bible?

The Bible is both a picture of what it's all like—or a guide, or an introduction, you might say—and a means of getting on with it. It's like a map in one way and like food in another.

Oh. Is the Bible the only way Christians find grace?

Well, they pray, for another thing.

Oh, dear.

You said that about the Bible. What's the matter now?

Oh, well, I mean—I really can't pray. It's such a drag. And it doesn't make any difference anyway.

How do you mean?

The same things happen to the people who pray and to the ones who don't.

Where did you get the idea that the same things *wouldn't* happen?

Well, isn't prayer supposed to be a way of getting God to deflect disaster? You know, "Dear God, please don't let it rain today," or "Let me have passed that exam," or "Keep me safe from harm." And then first thing you know, bam, it rains, or you find out your grade, or you break your leg in a smashup. You can't pretend that it works.

Um . . .

Um is right. It's about all there is to say.

Except that maybe there's another angle to it. For one thing, *asking* for things is the wrong place to begin. Maybe prayer is more a matter of beginning to participate in something—in the Way Things Are. In other words, *if* the whole thing is true—if the picture Christianity gives of it all is right, and God is God, and we are his creatures, and our experience here is more than just clutter, and it all has some bearing on what we were made for and where we are going—then prayer makes sense.

I don't follow.

Isn't prayer one of the ways a man gets into the right position?

You mean kneeling? Oh, I don't buy . . .

No, no. Or maybe yes. Kneeling isn't such a bad posture after all, if it's all true. But it's not cringing, if that's what you were about to object to. It's not a pharaoh-slave picture. By "position" I mean getting into the right *place,* where you can see what it is that is being pointed out—so that if there is, in fact, splendor, prayer is one way of beginning.

Splendor?

M-mm.

What splendor? What does this have to do with prayer?

Everything, I should think. That is, if things are just a random clutter, and there's no particular purpose or meaning in anything, then of course we are alone and have no obligation to anything besides ourselves. But if there is a great King, and if his majesty and splendor are manifest in our world, one of the ways of becoming at home in that world is to see and acknowledge that majesty and splendor.

Well, for one thing, I don't see much majesty and splendor, and for another I don't like this whole picture of subservience to some royal authority. You can't ask anybody in this day and age to buy that. Maybe medieval people, but nobody in the modern world.

That *might* be a case of so much the worse for the modern world. We would have to find that out. But "subservience" gives the wrong idea to us today. It implies resignation and defeat and repression. There was a time when men were able to see the business of bowing to another and acknowledging his excellence and authority as a noble and joyous thing. You might have a royal duke and a king: the duke, who was himself accustomed to having everyone bow and give way, brings *his* splendor and lays it at the feet of his liege lord. It is a duty, but at the same time it is an occasion of joy. The duke recognizes what all his own splendor is *for,* and bows before his king, whose splendor is greater. The king, on the other hand, receives that homage and responds with grace, raising the duke to his full stature again and investing his vassal, the duke, with the glory and authority of his own person.

You've lost me long since.

I know. We don't have any vocabulary to bring to all this any more. Our modern ideal of committees of the whole, and power struggles, and nit-picking equality, and chairpersons doesn't really get it. Maybe another way of seeing it would be to look at the business of applauding a great performance. Here there's no question of power or authority, of course. But it is a matter in which one set of people gives way to the preeminence of another set, and finds this "giving way" to be exhilarating and not a drag. When you rush to your feet in shouting applause, along with the whole throng around you, after having seen a fantastic home run, or a great performance of *Swan Lake*, or a play in which the good guy finally gets the bad guy, there's no question of "What a drag this is! Why should I have to kowtow to this guy this way? I'm as good as he is. Why aren't they applauding me?" What a miserable, pinched, unhappy frame of mind that is! The very going out of myself in that applause, the very forgetting of myself in the ovation, the very act of joining with the other thousands in accumulating as big a roar of joy over the performance as possible—that becomes, by a strange reversal, a source of joy to *me*. *I* am carried away. *My* being is somehow enriched and ennobled and fulfilled. By shouting "Bravo!" and clapping, I find myself, if I think about it at all, a richer, happier person.

Now would you mind telling me what all this has to do with prayer?

Isn't that one of the things prayer is about?

What? Three cheers for God? Who needs it? I don't, and I doubt if God does.

Put that way, no. But if what I've been talking about here is any sort of clue to anything, maybe there are whole vistas of joy that prayer opens out onto that can't be got at any other way. The prophets and psalmists and apostles and so on never stop calling on everyone and everything to praise the Lord, and sing to him, and shout with a loud voice, and offer up thanksgiving and joy and music, with trumpets and incense and gifts and . . .

Watch it.

Seriously. The picture in the Bible is that everything—waterfalls, the bottom of the sea, frost and fire and thunder, and all deeds of charity and humility—goes up in a shout of praise and adoration to God. So that perhaps part of the idea in prayer is that we get into step with all this joy that is already going on. You know—the Dance. Learn the steps; find out what happens when you try saying "Praise him." It might be one way of finding out what the sparkle of cataracts and the dots on a trout and the smell of spruce are all about.

What?

The Christian idea says that all this is a matter of praise. They really are praising God. That will never be discovered in a botany lab, of course. But botany doesn't claim to know what it's all *for*. It just describes what it all looks like from such and such an angle.

I thought prayer was supposed to be asking God for things.

It is, partly. That's another of the things that goes on in prayer. Adoration is one thing—subjects bowing down before a great King who really *is* worthy of this adoration. Praise is another—everything crying out in wonder and joy at the mighty acts of this King. And Thanksgiving is another—the offering of gratitude for his mercies and his justice.

Hold it. What mercies and justice? I should think if anybody took a piercing look at things, he'd be hard put to it to conclude that there's much mercy and justice in the world. That may be all right for the privileged few who have it made, but for the ordinary masses who have to struggle just to keep body and soul together there isn't a whole lot of obvious mercy and justice lying around. To say nothing of all the people who have to cope with leukemia or oppression or heartbreak and horror of one sort or another. How do you expect them to say much about mercy and justice—except to wonder where they are?

I'd be a monster if I pretended that there's a neat answer to that. I don't have one, really, except to point to the experience of the so-called "faithful" down through the ages. This crowd has hardly been what anybody could call the privileged few. But the whole lot of them—poets, patriarchs, prophets, apostles, martyrs, exiles, widows, paupers, and sufferers of every description—have somehow kept up the song of thanksgiving to their God for his mercy and justice.

All I can say, then, is that it must be possible to fool most of the people most of the time.

That would be one way of explaining it. Another would be to wonder if maybe they see something we don't. Maybe they've been gripped by something that remains unshaken in spite of their poverty and exile and pain. Maybe the poverty and exile and pain are transfigured, somehow, for them, and are encompassed by the mercy and justice that they give thanks for.

But that's nonsense. Here I am, a poor devil breaking my back in Ivan the Terrible's stone quarries, and somebody tells me that it's all really quite fortunate and that the old Czar is a dear when all is said and done, and that I ought, therefore, to stop my quarrying once in a while and sing a song of thanks to the old despot.

But isn't it part of the point of the Christian claim that news has come as to what the Lord is like, and that he is not like the Czar?

It comes to the same thing, say what you will. I mean, my load of rock isn't any lighter simply because you tell me that it's a nice lord I'm working for instead of a tyrant.

Maybe not lighter. But the picture is different. In the slavery picture, the slave has no real interest in what he's doing and the lord is interested only in what he can wring from the slave. In the Christian picture of things, the rock quarrying, you might say, with all its pain and sweat and fatigue, is part of the business of winning back through to the bliss that the Lord made us for—the bliss that is laid up for us.

What about the mercy and justice, then?

Wouldn't it be, for one thing, that the quarrying—or the climbing, or the sailing, or whatever picture one wants—has been gathered into the bigger picture, so that it isn't futile? Something is being *made*. We're *going* somewhere. The burden is there, of course—the burden of suffering and endurance and so forth. But help has come, and the promise that it isn't all in vain.

It would have been much more efficient, and much easier to see, if the Lord had just waved his wand and wafted the burden away. That would have been mercy, if you ask me.

Magic, maybe, or jiggery-pokery, but not mercy—at least not the sort of mercy that would have anything to do with the kind of lord our Lord is. Remember, one of the things at the very center of the whole Christian vision is mystery. Not efficiency, or obviousness, or magic, but mystery. *Why* he couldn't just let us off the whole burden of our humanness may seem a hard question with a hard answer. It seems that the drama has to be played out—that you and I slog through the experience of being men who have been lost and are now found, and who must go through all the steps of returning to that original bliss and freedom we left. But the process is a return, not a treadmill. Maybe that's part of what Christians mean when they speak of his mercy: this sense in which the "treadmill" has been transformed into a return. It is deliverance. And not only that, but the promise is that every rock quarried, every burden borne, is answered by some glory that is out of all proportion to the burden.

VI

The trouble with you, though, is that you're always having to refer it all to some great invisible scheme. It looks suspicious to me to try to make ordinary human experience and suffering somehow tolerable—or glorious, as you keep hinting—by reaching way off for some mysterious pattern or promise that makes it all look good. That's asking too much of plain everyday people. I mean, after all, most of us aren't prophets or mystics or visionaries.

I know. And the Christian view *does* have to keep reaching off to some pattern or promise, as you accuse it of doing. There's no way around that. But we've been head over heels in that from the start. The word that came to us in the meat-and-potatoes ordinariness of our history was the Word Incarnate, from outside that ordinariness. And any Christian would not only admit but eagerly affirm that it is only in the light of that *extra*ordinariness that this ordinariness makes any sense. So that to "accuse" Christianity of reaching off for some pattern or promise is a little like "accusing" a mountain of being high or a well of being deep. That's what the thing *is*.

But how is somebody who isn't a prophet or a mystic supposed to get hold of all this?

Faith.

Oh, dear.

Why oh, dear?

I knew we'd get here sooner or later.

Where?

Here. You trotting out faith—you know, "It doesn't make any sense so you just have to close your eyes and pretend that it does."

You wouldn't get a whole lot of support for that description of it from the people who exercise faith. For them it's much more like a response to someone they know whom they've found to be worth believing. Like trusting the doctor. His knife *feels* pretty much like the knife of the mugger, but nobody will insist that it's the same experience.

Yes, but I can see the doctor. You've never seen any visible evidence that the Lord is trustworthy, or that he even exists.

Visible evidence? That would depend on what I was looking for in the way of evidence. But you've come pretty close to the ancient definition of faith.

What's that?

That it's the substance of things *hoped for* and the evidence of things *not seen*. If you insist on some sort of "evidence" that will show up in a test tube or in a lens or in a courtroom, we can throw the whole thing over straight off. There are no angels and no Incarnate God and certainly no mercy and justice. Christians know that. They know they're committed to something that will forever elude any attempts to get it pinned down and analyzed in any scientific way. There's no getting around the sheer fact that faith is what is asked of a man.

But why?

Why? Good heavens! Why does the sea roar? Why does the thunder rumble? Why does the lark sing? Who knows? Except maybe there *is* something to be said. Maybe faith is the exact opposite of the thing we did wrong in Eden.

What?

The trouble there was that we chose the immediate and obvious and visible thing over the unseen thing—God's command and promise.

So?

So we lost everything. Faith does the opposite.

What?

It looks at, and clings to, the unseen thing—God's command and promise—over the immediate and obvious and visible. Another way of putting it would be to say that the thing asked of a man is that he respond to the Light that has come into the world—that he obey what he can't see.

So how does all this tie in to our conversation about prayer? About giving thanks for mercy and justice when you can't find much that looks like mercy and justice lying about?

Well, isn't it that the eye of faith has seen something that overrides, or encompasses, the "evidence"? Something that, in spite of all the poverty and suffering and injustice and pain—one's own and the world's—calls forth from a man a song of thanksgiving? I mean, this huge train of ordinary and extraordinary people down through the centuries: they weren't all crazy, thinking that things weren't so bad after all. Nor were they monsters who delighted in the spectacle of their own and others' suffering and sang songs of thanksgiving on that basis. They were in the middle of it like everybody else, but they saw and experienced something that made them full of gratitude.

What, for instance?

Their very experience, for one thing. It had been transfigured for them, so that it all seemed to come to them from the hand of their Good Lord, not just tumbling at them helter-skelter from some cosmic dump truck. They experienced the ordinariness of the daily round—dawn and twilight, sunshine and rain, spring and fall, air and sky, light and dark, the whole business—as gifts from him. And they experienced the bigger things—their existence, their lot in life, their vocation, their special joys and limitations, their very pains and griefs—as appointed by their Good Lord, and therefore as occasions for thanksgiving.

That just sounds mindless to me. "Thanks for this cancer, Lord." "Thanks for this suffering child of mine."

Nobody's pretending that it's easy to *do*. And I don't suppose anybody can pretend that it's at all like thanking somebody for some nice gift. It's more a matter of having been convinced that the Lord *is* good, and of responding— or of slowly learning to respond—to everything else in the light of that. The good and the bad—both somehow fit in eventually.

But I can't see that.

Neither can they. If they could, they wouldn't need to exercise faith. There's no getting around it—faith is a frightening demand laid on us. But it's not ordinariness that we're up against; it's the Lord. In any case, thanksgiving *is* one of the things that go on in the prayers of Christians.

But what about this asking business? It doesn't work, if you ask me. I mean, you're not going to tell me, are you, that if you ask God for something, you will get it? "Please, Lord, let me have a million dollars."

I should think the same thing would be at work in the business of asking as in thanksgiving.

What's that?

The realization that it's the *Lord*, and not some genie, that one is confronting. It's at least partly a matter of posture or stance—of getting into the right position.

What position?

Of subjects before their Good Lord. Of creatures before their Creator. Of children before their Father. In those situations, there's no question of feeding data into a computer, or of rubbing a magic pot, or of hoping for luck out of the blue yonder. There's a meeting of persons. A relationship between two personal beings who call each other by name. And of course, it's not just any two people or just any random meeting. It is you, in the depths of your being, and the Lord of heaven and earth—so that any asking that goes on is a pretty special business.

If the situation is as august as you make it out to be, I don't see how anybody gets up any courage to ask anything.

Nobody would, I guess, except that we have all been invited—bidden—commanded—to ask.

It must be a charade, then. I mean, if he is the Lord, and he is running the show anyway and knows what's going to happen before it happens, he isn't going to change his plans just because little me asks something. Is he? Is he?

There's no way we can even talk about his "changing his plans." That's all on the far side of a thick veil of mystery, and Christians don't pretend to have a clue as to how it all fits together. Christians are *always* up against mystery. Anybody is, for that matter. But Christians think that mystery is in the cards, so to speak, and that there is a proper stance in the face of mystery, especially the divine mysteries.

What stance?

Obedience. Worship. Submission.

But that's all so groveling.

I suppose it is if one has the idea that we're all equal in this universe and that *all* bowing is groveling. But if there is something worth bowing to, the people who refuse to bow are, of course, the losers. Christians think there is.

Is what?

Something worth bowing to. Remember, in old tales, it certainly wasn't a matter of groveling when the conquering hero returned and laid his trophies at the feet of his king. It was a noble and glorious thing, and the hero became taller by falling to his knees. But that's a picture of things we don't understand any more.

You still haven't explained how asking the Lord for things is supposed to make any difference—even if you do submit, and approach it as a mystery. It still looks like a dry run to me.

I guess the main thing here would be that Christians believe that, since they are bidden to ask, there's nothing more "unreal" about it than about anything else they do. Baptism, for instance: how can a simple ritual do anything substantial? It's all a charade.

That's what I said.

Except that the "charade" seems to be the point at which our world of ordinariness touches peculiarly on the world announced to us by the Incarnate Word. So that what *looks* like a pointless thing, or a dry run, from our angle turns out to be pretty close to the center of things. Christians look at prayer this way—or at the asking part of prayer. Nobody can come up with a diagram of how Cause A (my request) results in Effect B (God's doing something), any more than anyone can tell you much about the gynecology of the Incarnation or the trajectory of the Ascension.

Oh, good lord!

Yes, actually. It is the Good Lord. I suppose one way of saying it would be that Christians think the pattern of things really *is* hinted at in what has been commanded, and that hence the command to pray and ask really does have something to do with it all, and that the best way to begin to participate in it is to begin. To obey. The Lord whom they ask hasn't revealed himself as a capricious lord who likes to see his subjects dance silly steps for his amusement. After all, he *died* in our flesh and in our history. There was nothing unreal about that, and all these things that are commanded of us furnish us with some clues about how that flesh is being raised to his glory. Prayer is one of these clues. An asking-receiving relationship is part of it.

But suppose you don't get what you ask?

Suppose you don't give your son exactly what he asks, or give it to him *when* he thinks he needs it? Is that the end? Are you a monster? What do you tell him? How do you convince him that you aren't a sadist?

Well, he knows me. He—OK, I see your point.

Nobody can pretend to have a very tidy answer to the puzzles posed by prayer, but it is commanded, for a start, and it is clearly an activity appropriate to the Kingdom of Love.

How? I don't see any special connection.

Prayer takes you out of yourself, for one thing. You are face to face with God, who is as "other" as he can be. And besides that, you become involved sacrificially in other people's lives.

Meddling, eh?

Not any more meddling than a nurse is when she works to make you comfortable, or a friend when he helps you change a flat tire, or your brother when he gives you a hand with some difficult thing. It's all "my life for yours."

I don't see how prayer is, though.

Isn't praying for somebody else a form of the same thing? Isn't it a going out of myself, a setting aside of my own concerns and pleasures and a giving of myself on his behalf? It's a means of my participating in his life that isn't possible any other way.

Oh, I see: don't ask me to help you with money or time or labor. I'll say a few prayers, and that will discharge my duty.

That's about as close to the truth of the matter as saying that Christ was discharging his duty to us by saying a few prayers for us in Gethsemane. His whole life, including his death, was a "my life for yours" sort of life, and his prayers were part of that same great sacrifice. Our learning what it is to pray for others is one way of our beginning to learn the steps to that dance.

Hold it. Gethsemane wasn't any dance.

Wasn't it? Isn't my-life-for-yours the thing that the dance is about? Wasn't that part of it? And isn't our undertaking to help bear somebody else's burden in prayer another form of the same thing? It's pretty close to the center, it seems to me. It's one of the ways we begin to get used to the way things are in the Kingdom of Love. Imagine anyone in hell praying for his neighbor.

But it seems so tiresome. It's so much trouble—praying for people.

Isn't that what any activity of this sort looks like from the outside? Anything that demands skill and mastery is "troublesome," if by that you mean that it takes time and effort to learn it. I suppose walking seems troublesome to an eleven-month-old infant. But it would be a pity if he didn't bother, seeing as how that's what he was made to do.

It all looks suspiciously futile to me, though. It looks to me as though most prayers just vanish into the blue. I mean, Christians pray for peace, and there are wars. They pray for plenty, and there are famines. They pray for safety, and there are accidents. They pray for health, and everybody dies. It's not a very encouraging ledger. The whole enterprise doesn't make any sense, if effects are what you are looking for.

No more sense, I guess, than the Incarnation made. I mean, the Roman Empire went on its merry way, and sin flourished, and history got more and more chaotic—not a very encouraging roster of effects. But it depends on where you are looking for your effects. Christians believe that the Incarnation opened up our history and our life onto enormous vistas—vistas that don't show up in our geography and history textbooks—and that the drama we see going on here, with wars and sickness and futility and so forth, opens onto the larger drama, the eternal drama, in which peace overcomes war, and health sickness, and victory futility.

You're flying off again.

M-mm. As the prophets and the apostles and the Lord himself did. There's no way around that. The Christian thing *is* the breaking into our plain history, with its apparent futility, of the really Real. Victory.

So how does this tie in with what I was asking you about all these futile prayers for peace and health and so on?

It ties in in a couple of ways, I should think. For one thing, as I said a few minutes ago, it would be one of the ways in which we begin to participate in this Kingdom of

73

Love that has broken into our history—a way of experiencing in pretty daily and immediate ways the "my life for yours" thing. And secondly, who knows how it is that the great ascending volume of prayer that goes up from good and holy men everywhere and always is gathered into the scheme of things? That's all hidden behind the veil.

What veil?

The veil of mystery that cloaks the Lord's ways of doing things.

I must say I'm a little unhappy with the way you're forever dodging behind this "veil of mystery" business. It really does look like a dodge to me. I thought your big point was that all the mystery had been revealed to us—that Christ was supposed to have opened it all up.

Not *all* of it. Good heavens—we'd die of terror or ecstasy, literally, I guess, if we were hailed with the whole show. The seraphim can hardly bear the sight . . .

The who?

The seraphim. The great angelic spirits who look straight at the divine Glory.

Oh.

We'd wither. Christians believe that we got as much as we could bear in what God disclosed of himself to men by his great acts in their behalf, and through his prophets, and finally in Christ. But nobody claims that *all* the mysteries have been opened up. In fact, the more you find out about this "revelation," the deeper the mysteries seem to be.

So—about prayer?

My point was that what looks like prayer's vanishing into the blue may well be rather a gathering of this sacrificial offering (that's what prayer is, surely) into the divine purposes and that the "effects" will be gloriously revealed to us in the final disclosure of things.

What disclosure?

The thing the whole creation is waiting on tiptoe for.

Tiptoe?

That's what Saint Paul calls it. Expectation. Anticipation. Vigilance. The frame of mind that the faithful keep alive all the time. Obviously the thing isn't complete. Clearly there are loose ends and unfinished business, and it's all either going to grind down into futility or whir on forever like a treadmill or *get* somewhere. The Christian idea is that it *does* get somewhere.

Where?

Glory.

VII

That's another of your words. How are you going to get glory out of this mess?

By redemption.

Ouch.

By the whole thing's being remade. Made new. Splendor coming from the ashes, like the phoenix—or like the Resurrection, rather. That event, occurring in such a backwater in our history, will turn out to have been the bellwether, as it were, of the Whole Thing that's happening. The idea is that, in spite of how discouraging everything looks now, the Lord is, in fact, working toward his own ends, and that he won't be frustrated. Evil—with all the suffering and pain and outrage and futility tagging along with it—was the joker in the pack, you might say; but the game goes on. And it's not just the Good Lord playing it out with the Dark Lord; we're all in it. Nobody has the luxury of being a mere spectator. We're on one side or the other—good or evil. And the evil side is bent on destroying everything and fouling the pattern of glory, while the good side is working at building according to that pattern. All works of love, and all prayers, are stones, you might say, in that construction. Or, put another way, the drama must be played out, and we're in it. It isn't just that we watch the good versus evil struggle; we have to take up our role in it and go through the scenes. We have to experience in ourselves the agony and the ecstasy, so to speak. Nobody escapes. We can settle bleakly for futility, if we like, or we can take up the tools of construction and join the good. Prayer is one way to do this.

How?

It's a tool to help us participate in that building. A tremendous amount of the work that goes into constructing any building is invisible—lots of boring and puttying and riveting and fitting and so on. But the ultimate edifice can't be finished without all these unseen operations. The Christian idea is that nothing of all this is wasted. But beyond that even, the Christian idea is that nothing that happens anywhere, no matter how small or random it may appear, is lost in the shuffle. No sparrow falls without the Lord's knowing it. The hairs of your head are numbered . . .

That's just a figure of speech.

How do you know? A God who made periwinkles and shrews and earwigs might have your hairs numbered. But suppose it is "just" a figure of speech? What's it a figure *of*? What does it suggest? Anyway, the idea is that nothing is lost. If that's the case, no prayer is lost. No widow's tears vanish into any empty blue. No imploring petitions from parents for their suffering child or cries of the besieged on the toppling walls—none of this disappears. In that great Disclosing when things are brought to their fulfillment, it will all emerge joyously, splendidly, heroically as somehow bound up in the whole scheme. The widow has suffered her widowhood, the parents have lost their child, the walls have fallen. The drama had to be played out. The sparrow fell. Christ suffered in the wilderness and in Gethsemane and on the cross. The agony precedes the ecstasy. Death precedes resurrection. The drama has to be played out. Nobody is a mere spectator. We have to tread right through the steps. But the people who believe and obey the Good Lord, and trust his promise that joy and not nothing is the last word, and have begun to act on that belief by joining their prayers to the prayers of all good and faithful men everywhere—they will see where their prayers have "vanished" to. They will see that the little acorn they planted in the earth is now a great, splendid oak. We don't get the oak on demand. We plant the acorn—the acorn of faith, of good works, of prayer, of any kind of self-giving—and the scoffer says, "Right. Now where's your oak? Where is it? Huh? Huh?" And we stand there dumb, or mumble something about waiting or anticipation or vigilance. It's not too convincing to anyone in a hurry.

In other words, Christians are always waiting for something.

I suppose they are. But they don't differ from anybody

else in that, surely. Any farmer has to wait for his corn, and any baker for his loaves, and any child for his adulthood, and any merchant for his ship to come in. Planting and reaping, and the long interval in between with its hope and patience and vigilance, seem to be in the cards.

But then they can never really settle in to live life now. They are forever deferring things to some sweet by-and-by. Nothing but agony now. All the joys later.

No. No, no, no. Right there is one of the central paradoxes that Christians embrace.

What paradox?

That, for all their "deferring things," as you put it, and their expectation of some fulfillment still to come, they are of all men the most committed to the here and now. And not just the agony of the here and now.

That can't be. Christianity is always trying to pull away from this world and boost everyone off into some spiritual state of affairs. Heaven and all that.

But right there is the paradox. It *does* drive us toward "heaven and all that." It *does* raise our vision to the long view of things. But that has the effect not of pulling the rug from under the everyday flesh-and-blood world, but of deepening its significance.

How?

By placing it in its proper context. The Christian thing stands exactly in the center between the two mistakes men make about their flesh-and-blood world.

What mistakes?

The idea, on the one hand, that this is all there is to it—that there's no larger rhyme nor reason for all this flesh and blood—and on the other hand, that all this is unreal, an illusion, or something to be rejected in favor of some spiritual realm. This second idea is always a popular religious inclination. It brings with it the heady appeal of mysticism and so on.

But that's exactly what Christians do.

Not if they pay attention to their Christianity. It's not the Christianity in them that makes them do that; it's something else, since Christianity is a very flesh-and-blood religion. After all, it celebrates not only the Creation, but the New Creation in which all this is made new rather than being jettisoned. And it looks for the resurrection, which means that our *flesh* is somehow bound up in the scheme of things and not just rubbish to be shuffled off. And, of course, right at the center it has an Incarnation. Its God became flesh. That's a bad business for the spiritualistic religions.

You say that, but it doesn't always come to that as far as most Christians are concerned.

That's why the Eucharist is so central for Christians.

The what?

The Eucharist. Bread and wine. The Holy Communion. The Lord's Table.

What does that have to do with it? That's just one of your religious rites.

To call it "just one of" is a little like calling Christ's death and rising "just one of" the things he did. It's *the* rite, really. And it's important at least partly as a constant reminder to Christians that the Eternal has come to them in their flesh-and-blood life and that therefore that flesh-and-blood life has itself been raised to glory. Flesh and blood are celebrated there, not rejected. This is another of the means of grace that we were talking about, by the way.

In what way?

Well, in the Eucharist, Christians eat bread and drink wine, and in this action they both mark and participate in the whole thing that the Christian revelation is about. The complete drama is enacted there.

But I don't see how the act of eating and drinking something has much to do with "the whole thing," as you put it —much less how it functions as a means of grace.

It functions, in one way, like the other means of grace— the Word of God and prayer—by taking a man out of himself, for one thing, by bringing him face to face with the Eternal, and more than that, by drawing him into the operation of that Eternal in time.

Wait. You're losing me.

Me too. I mean, there's where you're up against the— um—mystery. In all these encounters—in baptism, in the Scriptures, in prayer, in the bread and wine—ordinary people are doing something ordinary—splashing, or reading or speaking or eating. And that ordinariness becomes, amazingly, the means of their participating in something extraordinary. It's like the Incarnation.

What do you mean, like the Incarnation?

Well, the extraordinary (Godhead) met the ordinary (our humanity) in the flesh and blood of Jesus Christ, and it is via that very flesh and blood that we ordinary mortals are raised to extraordinary immortality. The operation took place, you might say, at the junction of the two. Which is what Christians say is going on in the Lord's Supper.

You keep mixing up terms. Which is it—Eucharist, Lord's Supper, or what?

Any of them. It doesn't matter. The terms are interchangeable.

Oh.

Anyway, in the eating and drinking of the bread and wine, Christians see enacted, in a daily, easily accessible, way, *the* drama. That is, ordinary stuff is taken and offered, and, like the "ordinary stuff" of Jesus Christ's flesh and blood which was offered to God, it becomes, somehow, a peculiar—unique, actually—mode by which we commune with God. We come to God via his Son, who offered his own flesh and blood as a sacrifice for us; and this offering of his is kept daily present to our eyes in the offering up of bread and wine, which he himself commanded. He said it would be his body and blood to us.

In other words, you think you're eating his body and blood when you take the bread and wine.

Yes.

Um—I mean . . .

. . . it's so *primitive*, right?

Right.

And so unspiritual. Not very enlightened. Right?

Right.

Well, maybe the primitive religions at least saw something that the enlightened modern man doesn't see. In any case, Christianity doesn't claim to be modern and enlightened.

I can see that.

But do you get the picture of what Christians are doing at the Lord's Table? They are participating in the same drama that occurred when the Lord was here in the flesh. He won eternal life for us by offering his flesh—his "ordinary" humanness, you might say. And that act of his is remembered by Christians, and daily made actual to Christians, in the eating and drinking of this bread and wine.

It looks like mumbo jumbo to me.

I suppose it does. But Christians don't think it's magic. They think it's a mystery. I mean, *how* this ordinary bread and wine can be the flesh and blood of the Incarnate Word —it's a little like trying to work out . . .

. . . the gynecology of the Incarnation or the trajectory of the Ascension.

Bravo. You're a theologian.

But why do they call it the Lord's Table, then?

Well, it's a meal, really. It's eating and drinking with each other and with the Lord. We're invited to it. The act of eating and drinking has always been a particularly rich form of fellowship, or "communion," between people. There's something about having a meal together that the human imagination has always seen as being significant—something that goes beyond mere conversation or whatever. Breaking bread together seems to seal something. It's people partaking of something together—a way of recognizing and enacting their solidarity.

What solidarity?

Our solidarity with other men—with other human beings. That's what the Church is all about.

The Church?

Christians. The whole crowd of them. The Church is the place where the real human drama is enacted as it is supposed to be. God's original idea for man was that he enjoy freedom of fellowship with God and with other men. Evil is the thing that ruins that—the thing that spoils Eden and that builds Babylon. The Church is the place where men are beginning to learn how it's supposed to be done.

Oh, I see. If I want to observe perfect human relationships at work, all I have to do is look at the Church. Hem, hum, uh . . .

Hold it. I said it's where men are *beginning* to learn what it's all about. Nobody, I hope, will make any very brave claims as to how good a job Christians are doing of it. But in the Church there is proclaimed and celebrated the thing that human life is all about—life in the fullness and liberty of fellowship with God and each other. The Church isn't an *alternative* to human life, or an escape from it. It's human life as it is supposed to be, human life set free to be itself—free from the pinching, destructive, deathly sovereignty of cupidity.

Cupidity?

Selfishness. Grabbing. Evil. The whole inclination to *get* that makes us shove past the other guy and that dethrones God in our hearts.

I don't see why you have to bring in the Church. I can be unselfish all by myself.

That sounds like a contradiction to me. There's no such thing as a solitary unselfishness. It has to entail other people. And the Church is the place where that is the order of the day. It is, as it were, the Kingdom of Love enacted and exhibited in our life and our history now. It is both the anticipation and the present actuality of that great and glorious fulfillment and unfolding when all things are gathered up in Christ and sin and death are obliterated forever.

You're getting . . .

. . . rhapsodic again. But it *does* have to do with glory and splendor and joy. The Church is Christ's Bride.

Oh, dear.

What's the matter now?

It's not a very attractive bride. I mean, isn't it a slightly depressing picture? Or are you going to tell me that the Church is beautiful and marvelous and that all the best people are there and so on?

A lot of the worst people are there, actually. And she's not too attractive from most angles. But that's a paradox not unlike the Incarnation itself: *he* didn't look too much like what he said he really was—the King, the Son of God, the Anointed One of God. How could this small-town troublemaker be that? His story ended miserably enough one unfortunate afternoon. Nobody was swept away with how handsome and princely he was. And the Church is a bit like that. Her beauty isn't too apparent, although there is this enormous difference: his beauty was there, manifest in ways that the eyes of good men could see but hidden from the haughty and rich, whereas the Church beauty is nothing she has herself. It's all from him. It's his beauty given to her, and beginning to flower and bear fruit in her. It's a matter of her growing toward the thing that she really is—his Bride.

How does she do that?

By obedience. By following him. By learning what Love is, since that is the opposite of cupidity, the uglifying thing that has marred us all.

I still say I can do this myself.

To be able to say that is to have a pretty seedy idea of what Love is. It's no mere matter of giving in a bit here, and of being kind or generous now and again—or even of being generally decent. It's nothing less than being made over completely—dying and rising again. The demand of Love is just that—the utter going out of myself. It's what took Jesus Christ to the cross, and what will take a man to the cross.

Wait. I'm not going to be crucified.

Then you will never begin to know what Love is.

That's absurd. They don't crucify people any more, for one thing, and for another, why should knowing what Love is involve anything so ghastly as crucifixion?

Because the breakdown between us and perfect Love was so deep and so utter that no halfway measures will mend it. No Band-Aids or Scotch tape will do the trick. To begin in the way toward perfect Love is to embrace the cross—to know the experience of utter death—death to my whole *claim* to independence, which is the root of evil in me. Pride. That is what lies at the root of cupidity. That is what tries to dethrone God, and muscles past the other guy, and builds Babylon, which is hell, really. The cross was where the other principle—the Love of God—was enacted and displayed for us, and we have to go that way. There's no halfway measure.

But what does this have to do with the Church's being his Bride?

The Church is what she is because of the cross. Her whole principle of life is the life-from-death principle—the my-life-for-yours principle—that was manifest at the cross, and she follows her Lord in that way. It's what is celebrated, actually, in her central act, the Eucharist. Her nourishment comes from bread that is broken. Her life is poured-out life. Her beauty appears only insofar as she dies and rises with her crucified and risen Lord. You see ugliness and failure among Christians precisely because of their failure to be wholly identified with the Lord in his death and Resurrection. The old pride and cupidity are at work.

I should think it would be much more convincing if he would just make it a once-for-all transaction—you know: Bang! There, all your pride and cupidity are gone. That way the rest of humanity would be able to see what perfect Love looked like at work among people, and everybody would buy it.

There's not much more guarantee of that happening than there was that the people who saw the Lord in the days of his flesh would all buy that. They didn't. The difficulty is that it's not as neat a picture as that. It's not a simple choice between goodness and badness, with goodness always winning. For some reason, we turn out not to *want* goodness, really. That was pointed out a long time ago about Jesus: he was the Light coming into the world—the exhibition of what goodness was really like—and, instead of flocking after it, they rejected it. There's the trouble. We don't *want* it, it seems. And besides that, you say it would be much more convincing if it were all done in a flash—the church instantly changed into a crowd of perfectly loving people. Well, maybe so, from one viewpoint. But that's not the way it is. The acorn has to grow. The drama has to be played out. We have to experience the whole process in ourselves—the lifelong, daily drama of crucifixion and resurrection, of life from death. That's why the Church keeps celebrating the Eucharist.

Why?

Because that repeated enactment is the enactment of what her life is all about. The cross is always operative. Love always gives itself. Her life is always literally life-from-death. She has to learn every day the principle of my-life-for-yours, which the Eucharist presents to her. Her nourishment is bread that is broken. Actually, the Church is not only the Bride of Christ; she is his Body.

I thought you said the bread in the Eucharist was his Body.

It is.

That's too mixed-up a picture. You can't have a Bride who is her husband's Body.

This is like the other pictures we talked about before—

85

the way the Lord is both priest and victim, or conqueror and servant, or whatever. You have to get different pictures for the different things you want to emphasize at the moment.

Well, what is it you are trying to emphasize by saying that the Church is his Body?

That it is the continuation of his presence here on earth. He was personally here in human flesh for thirty some years a few centuries back, and he bore that flesh to his Father's glory. That's what Christians mean by the Ascension. But he is still here in human flesh in another mode—in you and me.

You, maybe. I'm not in this.

You could be, though. Anyway, the Church has the same task as he had.

What's that?

To manifest the Love of God in human flesh and to give itself for the life of the world. Or let's put it this way: his people—the Church, that is—have been summoned into the completing of that task which he began.

What did he do—leave it half finished?

No. He finished it, all right.

How can you complete something that's already finished?

It's . . .

. . . a paradox, right? A mystery.

You're getting pretty good. Yes, he did finish the work he came to do—the work of ransoming us and of reuniting us with God. That is, he finished it in the sense of accomplishing all that was necessary. But it's not "finished" in the sense that it is a closed book, or an event that occurred sometime in the past and is now over and done with. It is open and living—it is what history is about, really. Christ's life and death and Resurrection were the bringing to a point in time, you might say, of redemption. But he was the Lamb slain from the foundation of the world, remember. God's grace didn't *start* in Bethlehem or end on the Mount of Olives when Jesus returned to his Father at the Ascension.

VIII

So what is the connection between all this and what the Church is doing?

It is his Body now on earth. Christians are participating in, and carrying out, that work of redemption in and for the world. Another way to put it is that, just as he was the pioneer, so to speak, of the new kingdom—the Kingdom of Love—or of the new kind of person who would be at home in that kingdom, so his followers are pioneers for the whole creation. They blaze the trail toward the great Unfolding, and the rest of creation waits for this and watches it and strains toward it. It is the men in whom this new principle of poured-out life—his life, really—has been planted who carry on this task. They are identified with him, actually, in his death and in his Resurrection, so that they become the bearers of new life in and for the world.

But what do you mean, the rest of creation waits for this and watches it? Are you saying that donkeys and plankton and chickadees are an audience?

Um, yes. I confess that I boggle at the idea as much as you do, but that's what the picture is somehow. It was us men, primarily, who were redeemed by Christ; however, the rest of creation gets in on it too. Nothing is going to go down the drain. No created thing is lost in the shuffle—no sparrow, no nothing.

But everything does go down the drain. Think of all the donkeys flogged to death under crushing loads down through the centuries. Think of all the birds caged or tormented by little boys. That—and more—goes down the drain every day. And it's not just the calculated or heedless cruelty of human beings toward animals, either. It's in the pattern of nature itself. After all, a lioness isn't doing something bad when she rips the impala fawn from its mother

*so that she can feed it to her cubs. She's doing the same
thing that your mother did for you when she went to the A
& P. It's just that you got your meat in Saran wrap. And
every lizard that flicks out its tongue for a gnat is doing
somebody in. How do you mean, nothing goes down the
drain? The whole thing is a tissue of outrages.*

Touché. I know. I weep. But this is where the Christian
hangs onto *hope* . . .

*Oh, I get it—if we all work up enough optimistic feel-
ings, and concentrate hard enough on pie in the sky by-
and-by, we may be able to tolerate the sorry scene here.
Maybe things will work out.*

No. No, no, no. That isn't what Christian hope is. Hope
in this sense is a little like patience and a little like courage.
It is the means by which Christians grasp the reality of the
promise.

What promise?

That all things will be made new. That all creatures will
be in on the great Unfolding. That they will all dance the
dance with us. And this hope isn't based on any pale and
vaporous beautiful thoughts about optimism or sweetness
and light, either. It's rooted right down in the promise of
the God who came to us and went into the depths of all
this sorrow and chaos, carrying our flesh and bringing it
out again in triumphant life. You don't say words like
"Gethsemane" or "Golgotha" in the same breath with
words like "optimism." They have nothing to do with each
other.

*So how is it all going to work? Are you going to rerun
everything?*

What do you mean, how is it all going to work? How
does God become flesh? How does a virgin bear a son?
How does wine become blood? It's . . .

O.K. I know the next line.

It really is, though. How all this disorder, with lionesses
tearing gazelles, and boys tormenting birds, is going to be
brought to order, and how everything that has already
"gone down the drain" is going to turn out *not* to have
merely gone down the drain—how it all is going to be
made new nobody can in the least imagine. But Christian
hope isn't based on our ability to come up with a picture of
how it will be. It is based on confidence in the one who

promises it. And there's some sense in which the new life that is begun in us, and that unfolds in us little bit by little bit, by prayer and fasting and works of love—by the Holy Ghost's giving grace to us—there is some sense in which this seed in us is the same thing that has been planted in the whole creation. It bears its first-fruits in us men. We are raised to new life daily, and also ultimately in the great Unfolding; and then the rest of creation follows along. We men are somehow the uniquely chosen ones, God help us all, in this whole thing, in that we really do participate with him in this work—in the burden of suffering and in the glory. What the role of all the other members of creation is nobody knows exactly. It certainly *looks* as though they bear their share of the burden, and experience the agony in creation and nature in one way or another. But by the same token, they will experience the glory. They follow us. We lead the way.

What happens then? Does history just sort of shuffle up toward this great Unfolding you're talking about? I mean obviously something's got to change: the way things are going, all this will never come to pass.

Christians believe that Christ will return as Judge and King in the final act of history.

That's pushing it too far.

Pushing what too far?

The story. I mean, what is this? The Once and Future King, or something? King Arthur come back from Avalon? You can't expect intelligent people to buy that. What's he going to do—come riding down through the air . . .

. . . with ten thousands of his saints, and with angels and archangels, and trumpets and horses and banners and clouds of terror and glory, and all kindreds of the earth shall wail because of him.

What?

That's the way the story goes. That's the picture you get from the Bible as to what it's going to be like.

But that's completely beyond anything you can expect any sober and intelligent person to believe. Horses and saints and archangels!

I suppose Christians would say that it *is* completely beyond what any intelligent person can ordinarily believe. Like the rest of the story. It's all wildly *unordinary. But that's what the story is *about*—the invasion of our ordinariness with that unordinariness. We've been interrupted. Bothered. Hailed with glory.

But what happens then?

Judgment.

Help!

Help is right. We'll need all the help we can get.

No, but seriously. What's this judgment business?

It's all part of the pattern in which nothing is lost. No sparrow falls into oblivion, and no word or act goes unaccounted for.

What do you mean?

Nothing that has ever been done—by me or Attila the Hun or Saint Francis or you—will be lost in the shuffle. It will all *appear* and be accounted for.

By whom?

By you and Attila and Saint Francis.

How?

I don't know. The story calls it judgment—a weighing of everything, the good and the bad, and an answering for it all.

And Christ is the Judge?

Yes.

How come?

Because he is the *Lord,* for one thing. And for another, he bears our human flesh—he is one of us, you might say. It's not as though a complete outsider came along and acted as judge. He bore our flesh absolutely successfully, as it were—what Adam and you and I *didn't* do. He was the man who did, in fact, fulfill every jot and tittle of the Law, so that he is in a unique position to weigh *our* success.

Oh, dear—the Law again.

Well, call it Perfection if you want—or Love. It's the same thing. Anyway, the judgment calls for an accounting of our failure to fulfill all that. It's against that standard that we're measured.

So we're all doomed, right?

Right.

Thanks a million for the happy ending.

Who says that's the end?

Well, I mean—doom. There's not much more to be said, is there?

It's not so much what still needs to be said as what has already been said. What do you think the rest of the story was all about? Ask yourself who the Judge *is*.

You've already told me that. Christ.

Well, who is he in the story?

The Son of God.

And?

I don't know. You called him half a dozen things: Incarnate Word; God become Man; the Lamb of God; the Saviour.

The what?

The Saviour.

Oh.

So where does that get us?

It gets us to the end of the story. The Judge is not only one of us; he's the one who saves us. He is the Advocate, if we're thinking in terms of a legal picture. He pleads our case.

It doesn't look to me as though we have much of a case.

We don't. Except insofar as our case is his case.

How do you mean?

Just that. We have no case outside of him. It's a matter of what we're identified with. If we insist on being identified with the disobedience and failure of our humanity in Adam, we reap Adam's reward: corruption and death. If we are identified with the obedience and victory of our humanity in Christ, we reap his reward: incorruption and life.

But I don't see how it works.

I don't suppose anybody does. It's Mercy, really, infinite Mercy. Grace. It's the theme of the songs of wonder and praise of all the saints.

I still don't see how his case is our case. That sounds like a legal fiction to me. It sounds like jiggery-pokery.

It would, I guess, if he were just some random individual who had done some noble thing and we all decided that that could answer for us all. That *would* be jiggery-pokery. But that's not the way it was. Remember, the whole thing was *for us*. It was our flesh, our humanity, our nature, that he took on and bore and fulfilled and offered up in sacrifice —all for us. It wasn't some hole-and-corner thing. As a matter of fact, what went on in that story that was played out in Galilee and Judea was *the* disclosure in our history of what the whole show is all about.

What?

Exchanged life. My life for yours. *My life for yours.* His life for ours. So that when our flesh, our humanity, our nature shows up as a failure when it is assessed—or, let's face it, as "guilty," in the legal picture—and when the Trump of Doom sounds across our whole story, there comes an answering Trump of Mercy, his voice, clear and strong, which carries everything before it: "My life for theirs! That doomed flesh has been saved! Let doom and death vanish! Let forgiveness and glory and victory and joy appear! I am the Victor! I am the Second Adam. I won what they lost. I am the Saviour. They are in me because I was in them. They are mine because I made myself theirs. My life for theirs."

But who gets in on this?

"Whosoever will" is one old phrase for it. Whoever accepts his place in this whole scheme of mercy and forgiveness. Whoever doesn't refuse the dance. Christ and his Apostles certainly taught, with dreadful clarity, that it would be possible for a man to reject Mercy and to insist on being identified with disobedience and therefore death. There is nothing sentimental or fuzzy about the picture of this culmination of everything. Everything is manifest and everything is faced—all cruelties and defeats and lost causes, *and* all good works and acts of faith and prayers. And you and I face ourselves, and our attitudes and our works, and we answer for them. The picture is given in the story of a trial by fire, as it were. All the gold is purified, and all the dross is consumed away. Nothing is swept under the rug. There's no more question, say, of a cutting remark's being swept under the rug for the one who made it than there is for the one to whom it was made. That was a hurt in creation, a cruelty one man did to another, and it will be made right in the exchanges of forgiveness in the great Unfolding. Presumably, if the two men involved agree to let that evil be turned into an occasion of joy by the asking and granting of forgiveness, that will be done. But if either of them hangs onto it—the one by refusing to humble himself in asking forgiveness, the other by refusing to humble himself in granting forgiveness—then of course either of them may have to "live" with that forever as an occasion of death. It won't just be wafted away in some general fog of goodwill. Mercy isn't diplomacy or a matter of pretending that this or that didn't really happen. It is keen and hard-edged and bright-eyed.

I'm not sure I get the connection between this mutual forgiveness and Christ's case being ours.

Well, his case is made ours by our assenting to it—by our identifying ourselves with it. We do this by accepting it and embracing it, not just as an external item ("Oh, grand—his life was given for me, and that lets me off"), but rather as an internal, living reality. So that, as his life is given for us and we are forgiven, this principle of self-giving and forgiveness becomes the governing and life-giving principle in our lives. There's no question of merely *getting* something. Getting and giving become synonymous. It's what is being begun in the Church—in the whole effort there to learn daily what it *means* to be caught up into this life of his, to be citizens of the Kingdom of Love, to know the steps of the dance. And it's enacted and celebrated in the Eucharistic feast, where giving and receiving become indistinguishable—where what is offered becomes, amazingly, what is given back.

There seems to be some connection, in your view, between the Church now and this ultimate picture of joy.

Yes, there is. Because there's no question that a man can learn it alone. The Kingdom of Heaven—that is, the Kingdom of Love that was disclosed in our midst in the life and death of Jesus Christ and that will be unfolded triumphantly at his return—is a kingdom of mutuality, of the exchanges of bliss. There's no more question of our experiencing this thing in solitude than there is of our experiencing any kind of love—romantic love, say—in solitude. You have to have an *other*, who is the occasion of joy for you, making possible for you both the experience of *receiving* something beautiful (your beloved) and of *giving* something beautiful (yourself). It is an ennobling thing. One comes to know oneself as loved, and therefore as glorious. This is what the Church *teaches*, and what she's working at. That's not possible in a solitude. Hell is solitude.

Hell?

The opposite of the Kingdom of Love. Solitude. Boredom. Impotence. Wrath. Frustration. Everything, in a word, that attends the refusal of exchanged life.

But there's no such thing, surely.

Well—maybe hell *is* the ultimate "notness." Unbeing. The negation of all that really *is*. But on the other hand, it's in the cards. Christ talked pretty insistently about it. The paradox of freedom, you know: we are free to refuse, in the end. Hold it—I can't tell you *why*. I don't know the answer to that any better than I know the answer to why we should have been free to refuse at the beginning in Eden. The final mystery is no more gaping than the original one. It's the mystery of the will of God.

So you Christians believe that history will come to its climax in the return of Christ as Judge.

Yes.

And that there's some connection between all that and what we are doing now?

Some connection? That's putting it mildly—like saying that there's *some* connection between the acorn and oak. "All that" is precisely the great Unfolding of everything. It is this that Christian hope holds to and that Christian faith sees as the culmination of history—the history of the world and of every man's own life. The seed that Christ planted in his life and death and Resurrection back there in our story will appear now as a golden harvest. And the seed that is planted in us—that same seed of new life, planted in our mortal and sinful flesh—will appear as a golden harvest. And death will be swallowed up in victory, and cupidity in love, and sorrow in joy, and loss in gain; and then the dance will really begin in earnest. Oh—the shouting and the waving of palms and the flourishing of trumpets! What embracing and kissing and greeting! What bringing of trophies! What donning of purple and gold! What rolling back of clouds! What voices of angels and archangels! What rushing up of the whole creation in victory and joy! And what pealing of bells and casting down of diadems as the great King of Glory passes on his way, the victory won, eternal joy begun . . .

Watch it.

Mm. Sorry.
Do you think I could . . .
Well, now . . .